...gave one of the bundles to
...fied, she right away remembe[r]
...et it was wrapped in - the
... It was a Pendleton blanket
...present when the blanket
...e part of the bundle - in
...s when the country was s[o]
...o one could afford a
... blanket, nor had anyway
...ny company mill in Pendleton
...By some miracle the bundle
...ad managed to get there
...k. Now the blanket formed
...r wrapping of the bundle
...frayed, dirty, with holes
...s worn into it. Then it was
...such blanket in the country
...It was special. She remembe[r]

Back in the museum yesterday. In the basement. ... The Old Man sat cross legged on the floor and had [them] sit next to him as if they were in a tipi. He painted their faces. ...They were being recognized and brought back into the fold. He dabbed his palm with five dots of paint from his paint bag. Red ochre spots on an old brown hand (he's 81). He held his hand open to the Old Lady sitting next to him in her wheelchair, then he showed us. One for the sun, for the moon, for the evening star and for the morning star. He put the middle one on last. The middle is for the world, where we are now. Then he rubbed his hands to make his paint palette. His hands became the colour of his cowboy boots.

— Mike Ross personal journal entry for 13 January 1990

Weasel Tail

Weasel Tail

Stories told by Joe Crowshoe Sr. (Áápohsoy'yiis),
a Peigan-Blackfoot elder

Michael Ross interviewing Joe Crowshoe Sr.

NeWest Press

COPYRIGHT © MICHAEL ROSS 2008

All rights reserved. The use of any part of this publication reproduced, transmitted in any form or by any means, electronic, mechanical, recording or otherwise, or stored in a retrieval system, without the prior consent of the publisher is an infringement of the copyright law. In the case of photocopying or other reprographic copying of the material, a licence must be obtained from Access Copyright before proceeding.

Library and Archives Canada Cataloguing in Publication

Crowshoe, Joe, 1906–1999
Weasel tail : stories told by Joe Crowshoe Sr. (Áápohsoy'yiis), a Peigan-Blackfoot elder / Michael Ross.
Includes index.
ISBN 978-1-897126-28-8

1. Crowshoe, Joe, 1911–1999—Interviews. 2. Crowshoe, Josephine.
3. Piegan Indians—Alberta—History. 4. Elders (Native peoples)—Alberta—Interviews. 5. Piegan Indians—Alberta—Interviews. 6. Oral history.
7. Oral biography. I. Ross, Michael, 1950– II. Title.

E99.P58C76 2008   971.23'400497352   C2007-906745-X

Editor for the Board: Warren Cariou and Sylvia Vance
Text Editor: Carol Berger
Cover and interior design: Natalie Olsen
Author photo: Sylvia Vance
Maps: The Moustache Press, Courtesy Royal Alberta Museum

NeWest Press acknowledges the support of the Canada Council for the Arts, the Alberta Foundation for the Arts, and the Edmonton Arts Council for support of our publishing program. This project is funded in part by the Government of Canada.

NeWest Press
201.8540.109 Street
Edmonton, Alberta T6G 1E6
780.432.9427
newestpress.com

No bison were harmed in the making of this book.
We are committed to protecting the environment and to the responsible use of natural resources. This book is printed and bound in Canada on 100% recycled, ancient forest-friendly paper.

Second Printing, April 2018

CONTENTS

Acknowledgements
Foreword *by Jack Brink*   15
Introduction Niitsítapiiksi: Real people *by Michael Ross*   19

One
Buffalo Jump (17 July 1992)   35

Two
To the Gobi Desert (24 July 1992)   67

Three
Brocket (18 October 1992)   73
Ponokáómitaa: Elk-dog   79
Rattling hoofs   82
Centre-pole tree   83
Stopped in a powerful way   86
The Short Thunder Medicine Pipe   92
Sun Dance vow   96
Partial Crowshoe Family Tree   98

Four
Brocket (7 February 1996)   101
Vision quest   106
My dad gets doctored   109
One people   117
Talking about ghosts   136
Crow Shoe gets his name   139

Five
Brocket (15 February 1996)   141

Six
Brocket (3 April 1996)   159
Choosing my Indian way   159
Face paint   163
Ksisohksisiiksi: Mosquitoes   164
Battle with some Crees   166
Wolf Traveller's death   171

Seven
Brocket (23 May 1996)   175
Sun Dances   175
Bottle and feather   182
Where to pray   184
Tipi transfers   186

Eight
Brocket (27 October 1998)   199
Aissko'kiinaiksi: Ants   199
Ghost house   202
The haunted bracelets   203
Pokaamoiksi: Bees   204
A dream   205

Nine
Brocket (23 November 1998)   207
Longhorns   207
A closing prayer   208

Bibliography   213
Index   219
Map: In southern Alberta   229
Map: On the Peigan Indian Reserve   231
Map: At Brocket   233

ACKNOWLEDGEMENTS

Many have helped realize the Old Man's book. Certain people and institutions have been particularly helpful, and their energy, expertise, and endurance must be thankfully acknowledged. The Alberta Historical Resources Foundation believed in the importance of this project and provided generous financial grants from first interviews to final editing. They afforded us time to do the work, and Monika McNabb ably administered those grants. Glenbow Museum in Calgary provided in-kind resources, and staff there promptly answered my research questions whenever approached. Lindsay Moir, Gerry Conaty, and Doug Cass helped this researcher even when he could no longer physically access the collections. Jack Brink from Edmonton's Royal Alberta Museum breathed new life and personal commitment into the project at a key time. He shared resources and helped secure final pieces necessary to bring the book to fruition. Sylvia Vance respectfully and skillfully edited the material. Sybille Manneschmidt encouraged me in this long undertaking and, along with Reg Crowshoe, reviewed and commented on early drafts and supplied additional information. Brian Noble began the project and he, Reg, and the Old Man entrusted me with it. Reg's translation and cultural knowledge was invaluable. Lastly, thank you to Josephine and Joe Crowshoe, who graciously tolerated my questions, and for their trust, hospitality, and example.

ƒOREWORD
by Jack Brink

It would be hard to overestimate the contribution Joe Crowshoe made to the Head-Smashed-In project. In a very real sense, I am not sure this project would have been possible without his support. He greased so many wheels, spoke to so many people, interviewed so many other elders, logged so many miles on the road, and spoke so forcefully in favour of the project. Early in my archaeological career in southern Alberta, I met with Joe and his incredible wife Josephine. I liked them both immensely. They were at the same time intrinsically good people and also folks who wanted to improve the lot of fellow Blackfoot. We discussed the idea of developing the buffalo jump and how the Blackfoot people might be involved. Joe was immediately supportive and wanted to get to work. I couldn't spend the necessary time in southern Alberta away from my office, so I contracted an anthropologist from the University of Alberta, Rodger McDonnell, to work with Joe in the early days. Together they hit the road, talking to band councils and interviewing elders, all in an effort to do it right.

By the mid-1980s, Joe was already a man of considerable influence and respect. Once he dropped in on a Blackfoot band council meeting wanting to discuss our project. Typically, Joe had made no provision to be on the agenda that day. But quickly and silently people in the room began making sign language regarding Joe's desire to speak (sign language is still widely used) and in short order, without a word said, the chair recognized Joe. He rose to speak in favour of the Head-Smashed-In project. Few other individuals, Blackfoot or not, could have commanded this attention.

Joe's reputation was a formidable boost to the project. I soon learned that the degree of respect other Aboriginal people gave to an elder was closely related to how much that person knew about the traditional culture of the Blackfoot. It was common knowledge on the various reserves who were the great keepers of historical information. When any of these people were present in a situation where traditional culture was discussed, all the others would inevitably defer to him or her: "Let so-and-so tell it," they would say. "He [she] knows the *real* stories." Joe's reputation was such that others frequently deferred to him. But the other advantage of having Joe on the project was that he knew practically all the other Blackfoot who were widely regarded as the keepers of the most authentic information. Many were personal friends; those who weren't knew and respected Joe's reputation. Joe could call up just about anyone and say he wanted to come over and talk about "the old days" and off he would go.

Although Joe's involvement served as a great promotion for the project, this was an ancillary benefit. Promotion wasn't his main intent or interest. Foremost in Joe's mind was the need to use this opportunity to gather information about "the old days," especially buffalo hunting, from precisely those people who still remembered the most about it. He didn't care who the person was, to which group of Blackfoot they belonged, or where they lived. He wanted the best people who spoke with the greatest authority. The project was an ideal opportunity for Joe: someone else provided the car, paid the gas, bought meals, worked the tape recorder, and provided a small honorarium to each of the speakers. All Joe had to do was talk and ask questions of his esteemed colleagues about subjects that interested him deeply. Many of the people Joe interviewed in the mid-1980s are now dead, as is Joe Crowshoe. But their stories have been preserved as a precious record of traditional Blackfoot culture. Some of them are told inside the Head-Smashed-In Buffalo Jump Interpretive Centre. Also inside the centre is a room used for education, especially visiting school groups. It is named The Joe Crowshoe Lodge, and it could not be named more appropriately. I was honoured to write the text for a small plaque that hangs in the room, recalling the enormous contribution this man made.

During those years, and many that followed, Joe and Josephine became my friends. I shared countless coffees at their kitchen table, attended many Blackfoot ceremonies as Joe's guest, stood with him at speaking events, and was adopted into his family and given a Blackfoot name. One time, Joe asked me if I wanted to go with him down to the Pine Ridge reservation in South Dakota. The Sioux were bringing back the traditional Sun Dance ceremony, where young men put skewers through their chest muscles and then tear the skewers through the flesh. Joe, one of the most respected medicine men on the northern plains, was asked to come do the piercing. I was a little queasy about witnessing it all and even more queasy about being a white guy showing up on the Pine Ridge Reservation—a place that was having considerable political trouble about that time. I declined. Although I have since attended a number of piercings at Sun Dances, I deeply regret that I didn't take that trip with Joe. I'm sure it would have been an incredible experience.

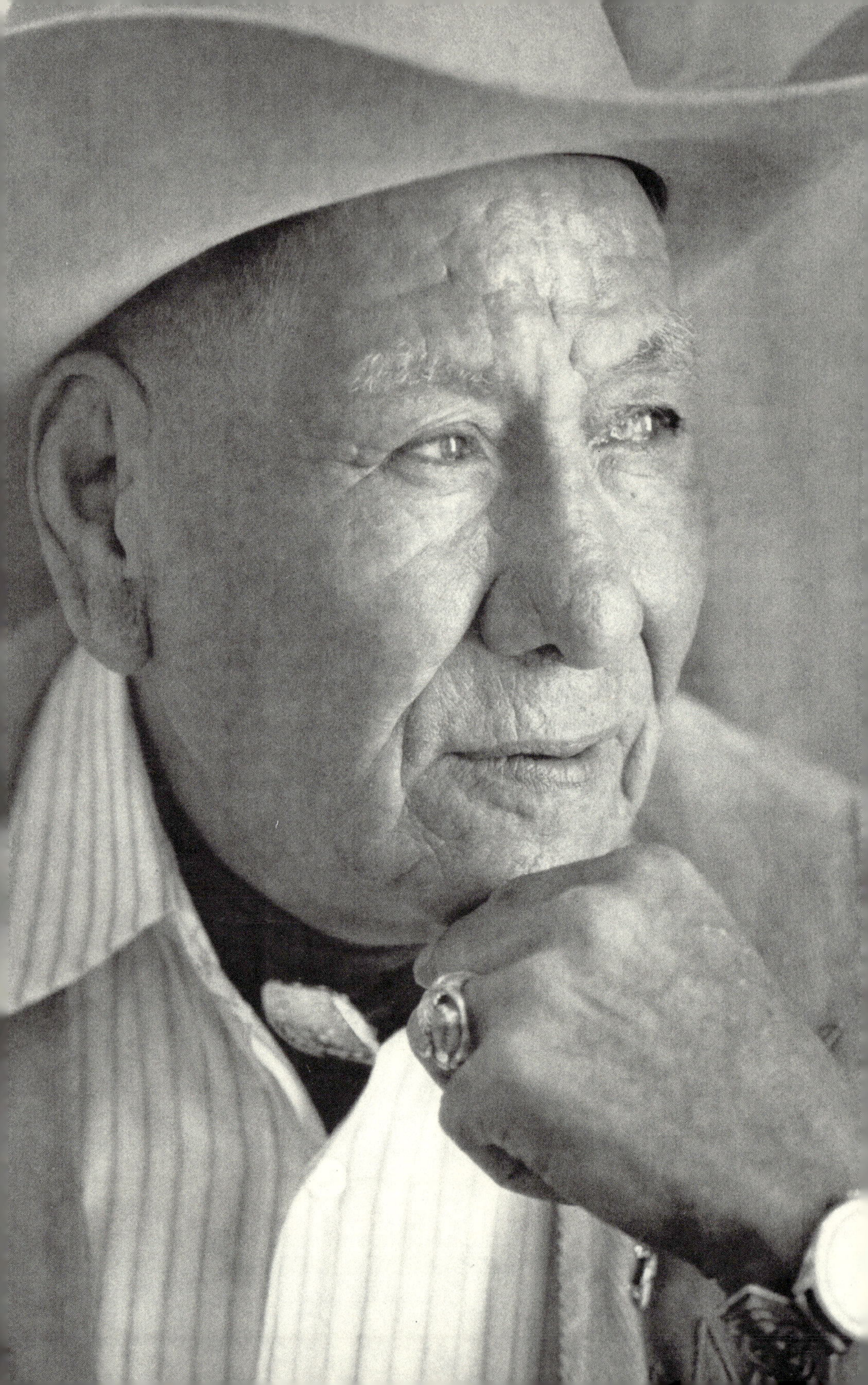

INTRODUCTION
Niitsítapiiksi: Real People
by Michael Ross

Joe Crowshoe Sr., respectfully called "the Old Man," embodied Native traditions and memories spanning more than two centuries. He lived a full life and travelled the world as an elder representing Blackfoot-speaking people. In his eighties, when he sensed his own circle was closing, he decided to tape-record some of his stories. "We're gonna write them down on paper," he said. This book comes from a faithful transcription of those recordings. But who was this man and who are his people? The following sets the Old Man's stories into a historical context of culture, time, and place and provides insight into the subjects he talks about.

The Old Man, Áápohsoy'yiis ("Weasel Tail"), was Piikáni, a member of the tribe known in English as Peigan or North Peigan, one of three Blackfoot-speaking First Nations in southern Alberta, Canada. The two other Canadian Blackfoot-speaking tribes are Káínaa (Blood) and Siksiká (Blackfoot). A fourth tribe of Blackfoot-speakers, Aamsskáápipikani (Blackfeet or South Piegan [American spelling]), closely related to Piikáni, lives across the "medicine line" in Montana. All four tribes share many family relations and histories, have similar cultural traits and traditional beliefs, and speak dialects of the same language. Collectively, modern Blackfoot-speakers call themselves Niitsítapiiksi, "real people" or "original persons."

On opposite page: Portrait of Joe Crowshoe, Sr., by Dan Riedlhuber, 28 August 1982 (Lethbridge Herald fonds, Galt Museum and Archives)

Beverly Hungry Wolf's *The Ways of My Grandmothers* provides information about women of her Káínaa (Blood) tribe in historic and recent times. Amongst her people's first-hand reminiscences are descriptions of beading, tanning, quilling, and the preparation of foods such as berry soup (Hungry Wolf, 1982).

The Blackfoot language is one of about a dozen languages in the Algonquian language family spoken widely in Canada and the United States. Blackfoot-speakers have lived on the northwestern plains for thousands of years, though their origins, westward migration, and precise geographical positions over time remain a mystery to archaeologists.[1] White explorers first came across Blackfoot-speakers in the mid-1700s in what is now central and southern Alberta and southwestern Saskatchewan. These people were warlike, did not use canoes like eastern tribes, and already possessed horses. According to their origin stories, the Blackfoot people have been here forever.

Before the early 1700s, in the so-called "dog days," Blackfoot-speakers travelled by foot instead of on horseback and had only domesticated dogs as beasts of burden: "Blackfoot bands moved camp about twenty times each year in a carefully scheduled round of peak harvests of buffalo and plants...[and] spent most of the year in camps of from ten to twenty lodges, numbering about 80 to 160 people."[2] During the winter they set up their lodges, or tipis, in sheltered, well-wooded river valleys.

Blackfoot-speakers were semi-nomadic hunters and gatherers who relied primarily on buffalo (plains bison) for survival. Other animals provided food and raw materials for personal, domestic, and ritual use, but bison was "real meat."[3] Two ancient hunting methods were to stampede herds of bison over cliffs called buffalo jumps or corral them in pounds. Niitsítapiiksi butchered and processed the carcasses and used almost every part. Bison meat—boiled, roasted, or dried—was a food staple. Boiled leg bones yielded rich marrow; some organs were eaten raw. A mixture of pulverized dried meat, mashed berries, and melted grease made pemmican, which was stored in decorated rawhide cases called parfleches.[4] Pemmican was a valuable trade item and provided nutrition in winter when fresh meat was hard to get. Tough rawhide made ropes, shields, and moccasin soles. Women tanned hides to make robes and warm bedding; skins were sewn together to make leather tipi-covers. Hooves, hair, horns, bones, muscles, sinew, paunch, and bladder had special uses too.

Women and girls gathered a wide range of plants and their parts, including bulbs, roots, stems, leaves, bark, seeds, and berries. Saskatoon berries (*Amelanchier alnifolio*) growing along rivers and coulees (gullies) were a favourite food. Saskatoons boiled with dried root flour made berry soup, a delicious recipe still served at many ceremonies. Ripe berries mixed with fat were stuffed into sausage-like sections of bison intestine. In addition to being used as food, plants had medicinal and ceremonial uses and mythological meanings. Indian turnip (*Psoratea esculenta*), for example, had special significance for Blackfoot-speakers, as this story illustrates:

The turnip (symbolized by a plumed headdress) was the plant that was pulled from the ground by the woman who married Morning Star and went to live in the sky. It was through the hole left by the plant that she saw her people once again; then she became homesick and at length returned, bringing with her the Naatoas [Sun Dance] bundle as a gift from the supernatural realm. The turnip had quite literally become a gate through which the connection between man and the supernatural was realized.[5]

Woman gathering berries, Crow Lodge, [Oldman] River valley, photographed by Walter McClintock in 1905. (Yale Collection of Western Americana, Beinecke Rare Book and Manuscript Library, negative #39002037297075)

Walter McClintock was born in Pittsburgh, Pennsylvania, in 1870 and graduated from Yale University in 1891. He moved west to regain his health after typhoid fever and worked in Montana as a photographer with an American commission looking into the management of national forest reserves. He met Piikáni, stayed for three years, and went back to Pittsburgh where he took a job that allowed him to return west regularly during the 1900s, spending spring and summer with Blackfoot-speaking peoples. McClintock wrote about his experiences and left over two thousand photographs now in the Yale Collection of Western Americana. He died in 1949 (McClintock, 1992).

Blackfoot-speakers have long used aromatic plants such as sage and sweetgrass in ceremonies meant to ritually cleanse and purify the heart and soul; they create the right conditions for receiving power from the sacred realm. Smoke from dried sweetgrass crumbled over an ember, called a smudge, wafts prayers to Creator in the above-world.[6] Plants and animals re-enact life's cycle and are woven throughout Blackfoot-speakers' traditional beliefs and practices, social structures, and stories.

Life on the northwestern plains was chancy, and Niitsítapiiksi knew starvation. Old winter counts record years when desperate people ate their dogs. Survival depended on co-operation, skill, and the sustainable use of resources mastered over hundreds of years. Blackfoot-speakers provided for their elders and less-able-bodied members; respect and concern for seniority and community are still strong values. They doctored themselves with herbal remedies, by mechanical techniques, setting broken bones for example, and through "healing practiced by individuals and groups who went through a formalized training ... closely linked to their roles as ceremonialists and holders of sacred bundles."[7] Long-evolved spiritual beliefs and religious practices helped maintain life, cosmic balance, and social harmony.

Horses and guns obtained from southern tribes in the early 1700s ended the "dog days" and profoundly changed Blackfoot-speakers' society. Moving on horse instead of by foot let warriors go faster and further and allowed them to gain superiority and offensive advantage over neighbouring tribes. Mounted Blackfoot hunted more effectively than before and the balance of labour between genders shifted: "Men now had more time to spend on ceremonial activities and needed more female labour to process their exploits. This led to a rise of all kinds of military

"A winter count is a traditional Blackfoot documentation of specific events happening in a given year, told at specific occasions or painted in symbols on a hide, something like a calendar" (Crowshoe and Manneschmidt, 2002: 5).

Bison killed in Smoky Butte region, Northern Montana Territory, January 1882. From a sequence photographed by L.A. Huffman showing hide-hunters' work and published in *Frontier Years* (Brown and Felton, 1955, 59–89) as "Five minutes work." White professional hide-men in Montana shot the last wild plains bison during the 1880s. They shipped hides for commercial manufacture into heavy coats, carriage robes, gloves and hats, and tough leather, used for shoes, saddles, and machinery-belts.

Laton Alton Huffman (1854–1931) was an American commercial photographer working in Montana in the 1880s. See also J.G. Nelson's *The Last Refuge* which describes changes to bison range, their near-extinction, and commercial uses of bison products (Nelson, 1973, 153–69).

fraternities, the dominance of male based societies, emphasizing the warrior as the ideal male image, and the size of families and subsequent role of women."[8]

The 1800s brought more changes. Fur trade increased contacts between whites and Blackfoot-speakers. Whiskey (*náápiaohkii* or "white man's water"), new to Blackfoot-speakers, was much trafficked during this time, with murderous results. At the same time, once-vast, seemingly inexhaustible herds of bison were rapidly dwindling, and had disappeared from the Canadian prairies by 1879, causing catastrophic

24

food shortages. In 1877 five tribes, including the three Canadian Blackfoot-speaking tribes, signed Treaty 7 with the Canadian government, gave up traditional territories and, eventually, were moved onto separate reserves, though the modern Peigan Reserve is smaller than originally agreed. The 1874 deployment of the North West Mounted Police to what was then called the North West Territories and the completion of the railroad across Canada in 1886 helped open the West to a flood of settlers and entrepreneurs. Cultural upheaval, starvation, and epidemics of smallpox, scarlet fever, measles, tuberculosis, and influenza devastated Blackfoot-speakers, making them virtual wards of the government.

During this period, white Indian agents administered reserves, doled out rations, and issued annual treaty payments to tribal members. Many reserves had resident farm instructors, although dry-land prairie agriculture demanded experience and new methods would take decades to develop. Piikáni also worked on farms and ranches near their reserve. Some homesteaders and Indian Department bureaucrats believed that tribal (versus individual) ownership of reserves, where members are part of a collective whole, discouraged initiative and held back "advancement." There were complaints that government-subsidized Indian reserve agriculture represented unfair competition. Racism and inefficiency characterized the reserve agricultural system.

Christian missionaries actively evangelized among the Piikáni starting in the 1870s. Canadian laws forced successive generations of Native children to

Crops first planted on the Peigan Reserve in the early 1880s were unsuccessful. Drought conditions began in 1886 and lasted about fifteen years. Peigan Indian Agent Harry Nash noted in his 1898 annual report that "climatic conditions of wind, drought and frost prohibit successful farming on this reserve" (Fort Macleod History Book Committee, 1977:11).

Carter's *Lost Harvests* describes prairie Indian farming (particularly in Saskatchewan) and Canadian government Indian reserve farming policy (Carter, 1990: 187).

attend church-run, government-financed industrial, residential, and day schools. A few of these schools, which seemed designed to take the Indian out of the child, operated into the 1960s. While some Native people value the education and training they received, the residential school experience left a bitter legacy of lost Blackfoot language fluency, disrupted families, abusive conditions, and lost traditional knowledge that would normally have passed from older to younger generations.

Most of today's three thousand Piikáni live on the Peigan Reserve. The towns of Fort Macleod and Pincher Creek are a short distance east and west of the reserve; Highway 3, a branch line of the Canadian Pacific Railway, and the broad valley of the Oldman River cut through it. Hay and grain crops grow on the reserve and fenced rangelands hold cattle and horses. The reserve's prairie grasslands rise west to the foothills of the Rocky Mountains. Blunt-topped Chief Mountain rises on the southern horizon in Montana. The weather is dramatic. Never-ending winds rattle the windows and warm Chinook westerlies melt snow and ice hours after a hard winter blizzard. Spring thunder signals time for a pipe dance or medicine pipe bundle opening ceremony. Lightning strikes close, and eagles soar high in hot summer updrafts off the Porcupine Hills on the northern edge of the reserve.

Joe Crowshoe Sr. was born in his parents' camp beside the Oldman River on the Peigan Reserve. He was descended from a long line of ceremonialists: people, who, at great cost, have acquired or been gifted traditional rights to perform various ceremonies held throughout the year. Ceremonialists learn the correct care, protocol, and precise use of ceremonial material and, when the time comes, must transfer it the right way to the next owner: "Ceremonialists serve their communities by keeping the spirit of their oral culture and beliefs alive. Their activities and behaviour are examples of how to live life according to Blackfoot traditions."[9]

Little is known about this photograph from the Ethnology Collection at the Royal Alberta Museum. A note with it reads, "Crowshoe from [Adolf] Hungry Wolf." It may show the Old Man with his parents in the early 1920s. (Courtesy Royal Alberta Museum)

In mid-life the Old Man became a senior ceremonialist among Blackfoot-speakers. He obtained his parents' Short Thunder Medicine Pipe bundle in the 1950s and held the pipe for almost fifty years. A medicine pipe bundle is a unique collection of associated objects, songs, and prayers owned by a man and a woman on behalf of the whole community. Blackfoot-speakers use sacred items such as various types and sizes of bundles to help Creator intervene to promote the welfare and balance of individuals and the community. Before he died, the Old Man transferred the medicine pipe bundle to his son Reg and his wife, Rose. Reg Crowshoe, himself a respected ceremonialist and cultural advisor, spoke in a 1995 interview about the dual physical/abstract nature of sacred objects such as medicine pipe bundles and of the vital role they play:

The bundles give you abstract authority to exist ... Historically, when we put bundles together, people brought material objects to come together in a physical bundle. Each item has a song, a protocol, ... an origin story, authority, what have you; ... an abstract component. ...That abstract bundle's got the wisdom, education, spirituality. ... Those are your rules for decisions to help your community survive. [10]

During his life the Old Man owned several painted tipis with sacred designs, knew healing medicines, and had rights to give sweatlodges and All-night Smoke ceremonies. He belonged to the Thunder Medicine Pipe Society, was a member of the Brave Dog Society, and, in the 1950s, formed the Red Coat Society.[11] Most important in the hierarchy of his transferred rights was his support of his wife, Josephine, the Old Lady, in reviving the *Ookáán* (Sun Dance) and in their stewardship of the *Naatoas* (Sun Dance headdress) owned by Josephine.

Joe Crowshoe Sr.'s spirituality embraced more than one religious belief and practice. "We're all one people under God. We're all the same," he said. He became an Anglican layreader in the 1950s but resisted pressure to give up his traditional ways. In one of his stories he remembered how Church officials told him, "Joe, go back home, gather all your bundles, your ceremonial stuff, and burn them. When they're all burnt you can come back and you can become a priest." But he refused. The bundles stood for his people and

John Snow Sr. (Stoney), Mikhail Gorbachev, then President of the USSR, and Joe Crowshoe Sr. (shown with his son, Reg) received honorary degrees from the University of Calgary in May 1990. (Courtesy University of Calgary, 93–026/7 #46)

this event confirmed his life's path, and, "years later, he was instrumental in teaching religious and cultural Blackfoot ceremonies to the community's younger generation."[12] He shared knowledge with the world far beyond his own community. The Old Man represented Blackfoot-speaking people as a spiritual leader travelling on cultural exchanges to Aboriginal peoples in other countries. In 1989 he received a Canadian Citation for Citizenship, an Alberta Achievement Award, and honorary doctorates from the University of Montana and the University of Calgary ("Dr. Crowshoe" was inscribed on one of his ball caps).

Josephine and Joe Crowshoe Sr. examining some of the newly repatriated Scriver Collection, Edmonton 1989. Published in *Storyteller* 10: 3.2 (1990). Alberta Culture and Multiculturalism. (Courtesy Royal Alberta Museum)

A Montana collector started the Scriver Collection in 1903, which eventually included over 500 items, much of it Blackfoot cultural material. Joint efforts of the Alberta, Canadian, and US governments repatriated the collection in 1989 and, soon after it was acquired, the Provincial Museum of Alberta in Edmonton invited Josephine and Joe Crowshoe Sr. to work with the collection: "During [three days in January, the Crowshoes] viewed the collection, purified the bundles in a traditional ceremony, ceremonially painted the staff working with the collection on a daily basis, and gave us their views on how the ceremonial material should be properly and respectfully displayed and stored in the Museum" (Stepney, 1990: 2), 2002: 14.

The Old Man and the Old Lady were married for sixty-five years, had twelve children, adopted five others, and, at the time of his death,

had forty-nine grandchildren, one hundred great-grandchildren, and four great-great-grandchildren. They often travelled to ceremonies, meetings, rodeos, and powwows throughout Canada and the northwestern United States and served their community for over sixty years. The Old Man and the Old Lady were appointed to the Order of Canada in 1991 and received Canada's National Aboriginal Achievement Award for Heritage and Spirituality in 1998. Joe Crowshoe Sr. was a lifetime Peigan Band Councillor.

ABOUT THE WRITING OF THIS BOOK

To make this book, the Old Man recorded about twenty hours of audiotape during the years 1991 to 1998, speaking both Blackfoot and English. Several years separated some taping and translating sessions, meaning that I sometimes asked in English what he had already talked about in Blackfoot on earlier, not yet translated, tapes. Compiling the final transcript was like piecing together a complicated jigsaw puzzle.

Brian Noble (who made the first recordings) and I are non-Native urban Canadians with world views different from those of traditional Piikáni. The Old Man's first language was Blackfoot but we do not speak it. He wanted to make his own tapes but this was impractical. He worried, justifiably, that someday, "there'll be no more Blackfoot [language]." The Old Lady always sat beside him at their kitchen table during the tapings, paraphrasing his Blackfoot words in English, reminiscing, joking, and exhorting us to "Listen to this!"

Converting the Old Man's spoken word to print was challenging. A text cannot match the sound of someone's voice, with its familiar pitch and rhythm. Sign language, looks, laughter, and songs do not come across. In print we miss a moving performance that is different each time. Translating the Old Man's stories word for word did not work because many Blackfoot language words and phrases lack direct English equivalents and the two languages have different grammatical rules. It was not always clear how to punctuate what he said.

When transcribing oral narratives it is tempting to tidy up grammar and remove false starts and repetitions — the way all of us speak. This book follows verbatim the Old Man's voice as he spoke English, but text translated into English from the Blackfoot language is in the voice of the translator. Translated text has been lightly edited to better represent the Old Man's first-language fluency.

Throughout the text, ellipses —"..."— indicate pauses, thoughts that trail off, and jumps in the original interview transcript. A question mark follows unknown words, unchecked facts, uncertain spellings, unclear names, and unidentified people. My own clarifications are set within square brackets. Most stories appear in the order he told them. Notes and sidebars tell more about subjects, people, and places.

Blackfoot-speakers' culture was oral-based and did not have a written form until the late nineteenth century. There is still no agreed way of spelling or writing the several slightly different Blackfoot dialects. For a formalized orthography I used Frantz and Russell's 1989 *Blackfoot Dictionary* based on the Káínaa (Blood) dialect.

Complete copies of project audiotapes and transcripts of unedited interviews are in the Glenbow Museum in Calgary, Alberta. Most photographs and images of copied documents reproduced here come from public collections. Photograph captions identify everyone possible: Native persons featured in photographs, mostly taken by white photographers, are often anonymous. Publication of some images may lead to the recovery of missing information and the correction of errors.

The Old Man suffered a stroke during the project, and his diminished stamina, hearing, and vision toward the end of his life meant we never discussed my transcription of the tapes or looked over the images I had selected. My growing awareness of what we were soon to lose accelerated the pace of my taping sessions and limited my preparation time. There was no chance to ask follow-up questions or check facts. But it was hardly necessary. He had a long and accurate memory. We ran out of time with this remarkable man. Joe Crowshoe Sr. died in Brocket on 28 October 1999.

Michael Ross

Edmonton, July 2007

NOTES

1   Brink, "Dog Days in Southern Alberta," 1986.

2   Wissler and Duvall, 1995: xiv. See also Nitsitapiisiini for a map of seasonal movements made by a clan of Aamsskáápipikani (Blackfeet) during the year 1900 (previously illustrated in *Plants and the Blackfoot*).

3   Dempsey, 1986: 404.

4   Robert H. Lowie's *Indians of the Plains* examines Plains Indian material culture and includes numerous illustrations of decorated parfleches (1954).

5   Hellson and Gadd, 1974: 8.

6   Hellson and Gadd, 1974.

7   Ibid., 41 F.

8   Ibid., 7–8.

9   Manneschmidt, 2000: A16.

10 Ross and Crowshoe, 1996: 248.

11 Joe Crowshoe Sr. memorial service brochure (no date or author), Brocket.

12 Manneschmidt, 2000: A16.

One

BUFFALO JUMP

17 July 1992

ON 17 JULY 1992 JOE CROWSHOE SR. AND BRIAN NOBLE SAT DOWN TOGETHER IN A TIPI DURING THE ANNUAL BUFFALO DAYS POWWOW AT HEAD-SMASHED-IN BUFFALO JUMP TO TAPE-RECORD HIS BOOK. THE OLD MAN SPOKE MOSTLY BLACKFOOT, AND NO TRANSLATOR WAS PRESENT. HIS SON, REG CROWSHOE, TRANSLATED THE TAPE ON 26 MARCH 1996.

JOE [Speaking in Blackfoot]: *Óki*. My name is Weasel Tail, Áápohsoy'yiis. Well, I'm going to tell the story about my life—the way I was raised and the way I lived my life. Back then I knew all the Indian old-timers from the Peigan land. Today things have changed a lot. Today we're camping here at [the Head-Smashed-In] Buffalo Jump. There's gonna be a big celebration. Now, also over in the Peigan land when I was young and the way I understood stories that were told to me, we're gonna write them down on paper.

Óki is a Blackfoot word used to get someone's attention, begin a statement, or declare greetings.

Óki. That was when the old-timers, the best of the crop of old-timers that knew our culture ... I [strongly] believed in my prayer. There were a lot of old-timers back then, but today there are not too many of those good old-timers left.

Óki. When I was born it was the Cold Moon month: nineteen hundred, ninth year. This is the time when nineteen hundred didn't have ten years on it yet, that was when I was born. Now, I am eighty years and three years. I was gonna start long time ago to tell the story of my life. I try really hard to make friends with all kinds of people—old people, children — I try hard. I had a good life that was given to me by the old-timers, the wisdom and the knowledge they talked to me about.

The Old Man's accepted birth date is 3 January 1909, though the actual year may be 1911. Church records show "Joseph Crow Shoes" baptized on 3 March 1911, "*âgé d'environ 3 mois*" (Oblate papers, Provincial Archives of Alberta). The 1923 Peigan Indian Agency treaty payment list includes him, age twelve, along with four brothers: Jack, eighteen; Arthur, thirteen; Richard, seven; and, Dorrat (David), two. His father, Willie Crow Shoe, was forty-two at that time, and his mother, All Listening, was thirty-seven (Glenbow Archives, M1826 f.11). Joe Crowshoe died on 28 October 1999.

Óki. I went to school at the school house, at the white coat school. I went to school there. I stayed there for a long time. I went there for nine years and I left the school. At the time of the big war [World War I], I knew a little bit about it. When I left school I tried really hard to help my father and my mother with their work, the crop work. We lived our life with horses. It made us strong. It made us not lazy, these horses. We had our life with horses. I'm gonna say this writing of my life in English, it's not gonna be too long.

The "white coat school" was the Victoria Jubilee Home Church of England Boarding School, opened in 1898 on a forty-acre site along Pincher Creek, two miles west of Brocket. The Reverend W.R. Haynes was the first principal of the school, which in 1909 had room for twenty-four boys and sixteen girls (Department of Indian Affairs 1910: 372). The school site also included St. Peter's Mission, a mission house, hospital building, and chapel. St. Cyprian's Anglican Residential School in Brocket replaced Victoria Home in 1926. See also Glenbow Archives, Indian Missions fonds M1356, and Anglican Church of Canada General Synod Archives.

Now, the holy things. I managed to hit the time when all the old people were bright with holy knowledge. Where we have Sun Dance today [is in] the east part of the reserve along the Oldman River. I worked hard at all the Sun Dances that I know of.

Óki. That was when holy articles started being transferred to me. The first time I was transferred, this young boy transferred to me the topknot of the Thunder Medicine Pipe bundle. That was the first transfer that I ever had of holy stuff. His name was Naatosiinihki [?], which means Holy Singer. He is the one that first transferred [to] me holy stuff.

The topknot transferred to the Old Man is a leather thong used by males to tie their hair. The tie is a physical manifestation of the wearer's qualifications as an elder with transferred rights in specific categories, such as a warrior, a holy man, or as a Thunder Medicine Pipe man. Blackfoot sacred objects, such as topknots, are moved from one caretaker to the next through transfer ceremonies. Crowshoe and Manneschmidt diagram the hierarchy of transfer items in "Akak'stiman" (Crowshoe and Manneschmidt 2002; Crowshoe and Manneschmidt pers. comm. 2006). Karl Bodmer painted several Piegan Blackfeet medicine men wearing hair topknots in Montana in 1833 (Thomas and Ronnefeld, 1982: 132–33).

Óki. And then celebrations. I joined as many of the rodeos and celebrations in those days as I could. The people then had a happy and joyous life. They were a strong people, the way they lived and did things. Well, I was told, "Listen to the old-timers; you'll get wisdom and knowledge, you'll be able to chart your life and know what you're doing."

Óki. It was in the winter when I left the school. I travelled a lot and went to many lands and met all kinds of people. I made it to all powwows and dances that I could make in different lands. There are a lot of Sioux songs that I know.

Óki. Now [1992], I am living a different life. I'm an older person. I'm eighty-three years old. I'm writing my life so that people would know who I am and know about the way I live so that my children can tell stories to each other about my life. I have a lot of children and grandchildren, boys and girls.

Óki. I have a lot of friends, white people [too]. I'm gonna be talking about the way things are today. I've been really thinking about my happy life back when I was young, my rodeo days and the times that I travelled. Well, when I got married and I stayed with my wife, that's when my life changed again. That's when I tried to get a tipi and a tipi design. I was given this Blackfoot lodge. It was transferred to me. I paid a lot of offerings on it. This Blackfoot person, his name was Fox Head. That's the person that transferred us the Elk design. That was my first home. In those days we had camp or Indian Days.

Some Blackfoot tipis have covers painted with unique designs first given by Creator to a person through a vision or dream. Each design is named and some are very old. Such painted tipis are considered sacred and have strict protocols concerning their transfer to subsequent owners. They represent only a small proportion of the number of tipis in existence: "The number of such painted tipis has always been small, probably about ten percent of all tipis were decorated in this manner" (Brasser, 1978: 8).

Indian Days, Brocket, 1924. Likely photographed by Peigan Indian Agent Chester Arthur. (Glenbow Archives, PA 3280–5)

One

I camped at the entrance where we collected money with that tipi. At that time, when I had the Elk design, it was a bachelor home. I didn't have a wife yet. And then when I got married [28 June 1934] I got the Buffalo Hoof design. The Race Horse Society, it was their lodge and I went and I took a pipe to present it to them and they accepted and they gave me the home. Today I still own the Buffalo Hoof design lodge.

I tried really hard, especially in the old days, on my raising grain, farming. Then my father passed away in the [nineteen-]fifties. In the wintertime, that's when my dad passed away, that's when I took his Thunder Medicine Pipe. The name of it is Little, or Small, Thunder Medicine Pipe bundle. Today I still have it. I still look after it. I still hold the ceremony for Thunder Medicine Pipe. I never let go of the sacred wisdom, the smudge and the prayers of our people.

The Old Man's father, Willie Crow Shoes, with Chicken Dance Society staff at Indian Days, Brocket c.1924. Probably photographed by Chester Arthur, who was Peigan Indian agent at the time. (Glenbow Archives, PA 3280-6)

All bundles are physical manifestations of a group's vision of survival. The objects in the bundles signify different aspects of that vision (Crowshoe and Manneschmidt, pers. comm. 2006). "Through the ages the naa-to-yi-ta-piiksi, or Spirit Beings, took pity on our ancestors and came to help them. Naa-to-yi-ta-piiksi changed themselves into human form and taught our ancestors the ceremonies and songs that we could use to call on them for help. Naa-to-yi-ta-piiksi also gave our ancestors physical objects that are now kept together in sacred bundles. These bundles are our connection to the naa-to-yi-ta-piiksi, and we use them in our ceremonies" (The Blackfoot Gallery Committee, 2001: 13).

Well, I'm telling about the old times when I was looking after my grandparents and people, and when I first stayed with my wife, when we started raising our family, our kids. I really cared for and love my kids. I took my wife around; I took her to different places. To Nez Percé land, to the far away Nez Percé people. That is where she's from. That is her people. I used to take my wife to that area so she can meet her relatives. And I wanted so much to live a good and happy life, me and my wife.

Encroachment into traditional Nez Percé territory by Christian missionaries, miners, and white settlers led to conflicts between Nez Percé and the US Army beginning in the 1860s and culminating with the 'Nez Percé War' of 1877. After a series of bloody encounters during a 2,700-kilometre flight, a small group of Nez Percé led by Chief White Bird escaped to Canada and, by 1880, had temporarily settled near Pincher Creek (Dempsey 1993). Some Nez Percé intermarried with Peigans (*Pincher Creek Echo*, 12 September 1995). Josephine Crowshoe, Pohkomaniitapatii (From Far Away Nez Percé Woman), descended from the famous Nez Percé Chief Joseph through her paternal grandfather, Joseph Warrior (Soo Woo), who married her Peigan grandmother, Suzette Can't Get a Horse (Kata' inim' ahi) (Crowshoe and Manneschmidt, personal communication, 2006).

One

Well, we've lived a long and good life. Now we've both reached old age. She's also up in age. When I left school my dad gave me his farmland, and today I'm still living on that farmland. And I raised my kids and children and we lived a good life. We pray so that we can be old and grow old and wise and raise our children and our grandchildren on this land.

Well, I worked also for the holy white people [Anglican Church]. They sent me down east to another province and I found out that our Indian way of sacred ways was strong. That's when I went back to our Indian way of praying. The holy white people didn't say too much to me about it. They were glad in later years that I went back to my traditional way of praying. We have a need to preserve our life as Indian people.

I also stayed a long time at the school and they taught me in the good way to learn to read and write and all these things that we eat, all different things. Now, we don't get any more to eat of these things that the old people used to eat: pemmican, fat, or marrow. Today, we don't eat those things. We all are white people today. We eat white people food. We all think the white way. The young people all think the white way.

I knew the old days. The Peigan people were wealthy. They had a lot of cattle and horses. We used to have round-ups. We'd round up the cattle. Right now, where I stay here, the buffalo jump is to the [north] of us. Back in the old days this is where our people used to get something to eat. They used to run the buffalo over the buffalo jump. This is where they had a good life, a life full of good luck. Now people

---

The Old Man was a layreader, an officially recognized but unordained person who plays a support role to the clergy by participating in certain activities such as reading parts of the church service, taking prayers, helping run baptisms, and officiating at funerals.

The "Jump" is the Alberta government-funded Head-Smashed-In Buffalo Jump Interpretive Centre, built into sandstone cliffs near Fort Macleod and opened in 1987. The Old Man was instrumental in preserving the site of Head-Smashed-In Buffalo Jump and served as its initial cultural and spiritual advisor. People put up a tipi village every July at the centre's annual Buffalo Days powwow.

come to see this buffalo jump from all over the place, and now they're gonna have a celebration here at the Jump. People are putting up their tipis and they're all thinking joyous thoughts and [of] good times.

O.C. Edwards at Head-Smashed-In Buffalo Jump, a kill site used for over 5,500 years. Photographed on 24 August 1912 by an unknown photographer. (Glenbow Archives, NA 4035-9)

Dr. Oliver Cromwell Edwards (1847–1915) practiced medicine in Fort Macleod for members of the Blood and Peigan Reserves for the last eleven years of his life. He photographed Native people and collected Native artifacts throughout what later became the province of Alberta. His widow, Henrietta, later sold his collection to the University of Alberta. Henrietta Muir Edwards (1849–1931) was one of the Famous Five women who fought and won a landmark 1929 court decision establishing women's rights as persons under Canadian law (University of Alberta, Oliver Cromwell Edwards fonds, and Glenbow Museum Archives, Edwards, Gardiner family fonds). Neither male nor female status Indians were granted the right to vote in Canadian federal elections until 1960 (Milloy 1999).

Well, there were a lot of those old-timers [there] when I got transferred my Thunder Medicine Pipe bundle. These are some of the people that paid the horses, offerings on my medicine pipe bundle transfer. Today, after all these years, I'm still living with the Short Thunder Medicine Pipe bundle. I always visit all the medicine pipe bundles that I can get to: in the States; in the Bloods; here, the Peigan;

Gleichen [Blackfoot]. I open bundles for other people. I know whatever the old-timers have given me in sacred knowledge to open bundles. Also the Sun Dance. I had to work ... to run the Sun Dance. All the sacred stuff. I work and keep busy at them because I feel compassion for Peigan people, Blackfoot people. I cherish young people, especially the ones who are going to carry on in the future our way of life.

The Old Man's maternal great-grandfather, Natoo-si iniipa (Brings Down the Sun) (c.1831–1909), also known as Apisomakau (Running Wolf or Wolf Traveller), was a renowned warrior and ceremonialist and was chief of the Lone Fighters clan. He had four wives: Nam'itsi'piaki (Went in There for No Reason); Natoo'kinimaki (Catching Them Two at the Time Woman); Sistts'i (Little Bird [the Old Man's great-grandmother]); and Itsipiawayaki (?) (Reg Crowshoe to Sybille Manneschmidt, personal communication, January 2006). He is referred to throughout this text as Brings Down the Sun.

The Old Man provides a blessing to an archaeological crew digging at Head-Smashed-In Buffalo Jump, c.1991. (Courtesy Royal Alberta Museum)

The Old Man served on the Piikáni Nation Council 1951–1979 and was made a Lifetime Counsellor.

Óki. This other thing I was asked, "How did the old people teach you?" I went to school and that's when I first spoke English, the white man's language. That's when I was taught to write the white man's writing. That was something that was useful that I used. When I grew older, I was elected to become a leader, a counsellor. That's when the old-timers really started talking to me so that I would pity all of our people because I'm gonna become a leader, I'm gonna become counsellor. That's when I tried really hard. They were teaching me with the sacred knowledge all these dangerous things and [telling me about] places where wrong things and fights might happen. Yeah, the old people really warned me and I kept listening to them as much as I can. I lived a very good life with the knowledge that they gave me and I took pity on people. I became a person that was gentle and I pitied my children. The way I care for my children is the way I care for people and the elders.

The holy songs, the way we handle sacred items — they taught me all these things. They told me to try hard at these sacred ways because in the future you're going to be working this kind of holy ways. This Sweat of mine, the Sun Dance, the Thunder Medicine Pipe, the blessing of painting faces, the offerings — they taught me all these things. And ceremonies. I really enjoyed them and liked them. But there was a lot that I paid for getting all these teachings. I had to pay every step of the way on these holy ways. I had to make an offering and a payment for every holy item that was taught to me. Now I'm starting to collect back what I paid. That's what the Old People told me,

One

"In the future you're going to be collecting back all the stuff that you've spent on what you're learning now." Today, I really value our sacred ways. I pray for people who are sick, to get them to get better. I pray for people who seek our Thunder Medicine Pipe bundle for survival and safety. They have survived from it and they know it. They get saved and survive by our sacred ways, the way Creator taught us.

Óki. Today these young people, they're kind of hard to teach these sacred ways. At the time of the signing of Treaty 7, it was an important point. The old people, they really honour the five-dollar treaty payment they used to get. They used to have a big celebration day. They would have foot races and powwows and really have a good celebration.

Treaty 7 was signed by headmen of the Blackfoot, Blood, Peigan, Sarcee, and Stoney tribes in 1877 at Blackfoot Crossing on what is now the Blackfoot Reserve. Since then, regular members of the tribes party to the treaty are paid five dollars annually. The counsellors were given fifteen dollars and the chief, twenty-five. The Canadian artist Edmund Morris noted treaty day in his diary for 8 October 1909: "We all drive to Brocket. It is Treaty payment — all the Indians present. I take the names of those I will use for [portrait] models. In the afternoon they have sports — riding horseback, & the Treaty money soon goes to betting. ... After, they will all go to [Fort] Macleod & Pincher [Creek] to have sports and spend money on clothes & c" (Fitz-Gibbon, 1985: 114).

The painting of faces: Right now, where I am sitting, this tipi that's half red and half yellow ["Where the Seven Brothers Lived" tipi design], is my son Deer Chief's lodge. Awakasina [Reg Crowshoe] got that lodge from his father-in-law [Julius English]. ... I'm glad that he honoured it and took it. That's why I pray for him, to try hard. I sang a song for him on this lodge myself. When we were all sitting in here I sang for my son. I was painting his face on this tipi design.

There's a lot that I want to talk to you about. ... I'm going to tell about the old people only up to this point. They taught me the way my life was supposed to be, the way I'm supposed to live. I lived my life a good way. Old people, I listened to them. It's good for all other people to be listening to old-timers. If you think for yourself, it's not wise. We need the advice of our older people because they have experienced life and they pass on guiding ways. *Óki*, that's it.

Óki. This morning we slept here, Crow Tail Feathers, Mai'stooh'sooa'tsis [Brian Noble] and I, in this small tipi, the Buffalo Hoof design, here at Head-Smashed-In Buffalo Jump. Now, what I talked about at the beginning I'm going to talk about it some more. Today, there are a lot of houses, but there were many years when we had to live out in the open land, camping around. We were camping around along the Oldman River, on the prairies, where there was a lot of wood and shelter and trees.

Óki. Here it was really good. The times that I had hard luck made me strong. I wasn't a special child or a wealthy child. Now I'm thinking back on my life so that my children can hear the way I was raised, and my wife too.

The Old Man is pointing out that he was not an *inii'pokaa* (or *minipoka*), a spoiled, special, or favourite child: "It was a tradition ... for parents or grandparents to select a child as a favorite, one who showed particular promise to succeed ... If the parents of a minipoka [inii'pokaa] went to many ceremonies, the child was likely to grow up to become a ceremonial leader. If the parents went to many social functions, the child was likely to learn much about leadership. Other minipokaiks, however, were simply spoiled and pampered so that they grew up expecting others to help them at the first sign of difficulty" (Hungry Wolf, 1977: 119).

Now I'm going to talk about along the Oldman River where we used to live along the Wolf Flats east of here, and Grassy Water, the Old Man [a cousin]. That's where we used to stay. That's where we used to go live at the wintertime. Many Rifle Man, he was there.

One

Those were the people that were sent to school down east. Many Rifle Man was one of the people that got sent to school in Onion Lake, Saskatchewan. That's where he went to school. He was there. He was also a policeman [RNWMP]. This [other] police, his name was Sarcee Man, didn't go to school. He was one of the people responsible for putting the whole Peigan Reserve in order. Right now we all honour Sarcee Man. He was a policeman. He pitied us, even though [he was] a young person like myself.

Grassy Water, North Peigan, in an automobile, 1930. Photographed by D. Cadzow, Auburn, New York. (Glenbow Archives, NA 2908-4) Probably taken by Donald A. Cadzow (1894–1960), who photographed First Nations subjects in Alberta, Saskatchewan, and the Northwest Territories during the period 1919–1926. He led the early 1930s Cambridge (UK) Canadian Northwest Expedition survey which collected over five hundred objects, primarily from Plains Cree and Piikani for Cambridge University. Cadzow's photographs are in the collection of the Smithsonian Institution's National Museum of the American Indian Paper Archive.

Standing: Sarcee Man, Tough Bread, Chief in the Timbers (otherwise known as One Eye Jack). Seated: Mortimer Eagle Tail Feathers (Indian name Ak-Si-Na, meaning Two Guns), interpreter; Sgt. D. Mason; unnamed Peigan interpreter. Photographed at Fort Macleod in 1911 on the occasion of the Duke of Connaught's visit. Originally in *RCMP Quarterly* 22: 3, 1957: 238. Reprinted with permission from the *Quarterly*.

This other man was White Cow. He used to drown [dunk] children. He was the cause of old people and people's homes to live in harmony because he disciplined the children and drowning was one of the ways. Young people were dipped, or drowned, in the river for a while if they didn't behave. So they were disciplined in that way. Soon as old people say, "Here comes White Cow," all the young people would hide from him. If you didn't listen and you needed discipline, he'll grab you and he'll throw you right into the river even if it was in the midst of winter and there's ice along the river.

It was a good life back then ... a survival life. Well, in the summer, when the berries were ripe, the people that we lived with along the Oldman River picked berries along the Oldman River. ... They would camp where there were a lot of berries, ... and the kids, the boys and girls, would all go in the bushes and start picking. The men would go out hunting deer and other game. They would bring it home. We had a lot of berries and game meat and used it for survival in the winter. Then, some of us young boys, we went along the river and fished. ...We had a lot of use for the Oldman River.

Today [1992], governments are trying to take it away from us. In the trees we used to move home, back into the trees. And back in the trees for shelter where our home was, was an abundance that was brought home. There were a lot of berries, a lot of fish, a lot of game. Today we hardly ever get a taste of good dry meat.

Óki. We used to haul a lot of wood. We start chopping wood in the bushes, and we used to haul wood for the winter. January and February, those were cold moons. We made sure we had a lot of wood chopped and prepared for those months. We looked after horses. We make sure we fatten them up so that we can have use of the horse all winter. The old people back then had a good survival life. There weren't any bad times. Everybody helped each other survive.

Now, dances. Our places where we used to have dances weren't like over here where we have dances today. ...We used to have a dance place where the No. 3 Highway goes up at the graveyard just west [of Brocket]. I know that place. The old people from the old times did a lot of dancing. We always used to walk up to that place. We used to put our lunches in a sleigh and drag them up to the place where we're gonna powwow. And you just see trails towards this place in the winter going up to this dance place. The name of the place is Where Crow Eagle Dances. People used to all walk there to have a dance. They used to have good dances. They'd dance all night. They wouldn't quit early. Today, we have good places for dances but everybody's sent home at midnight.

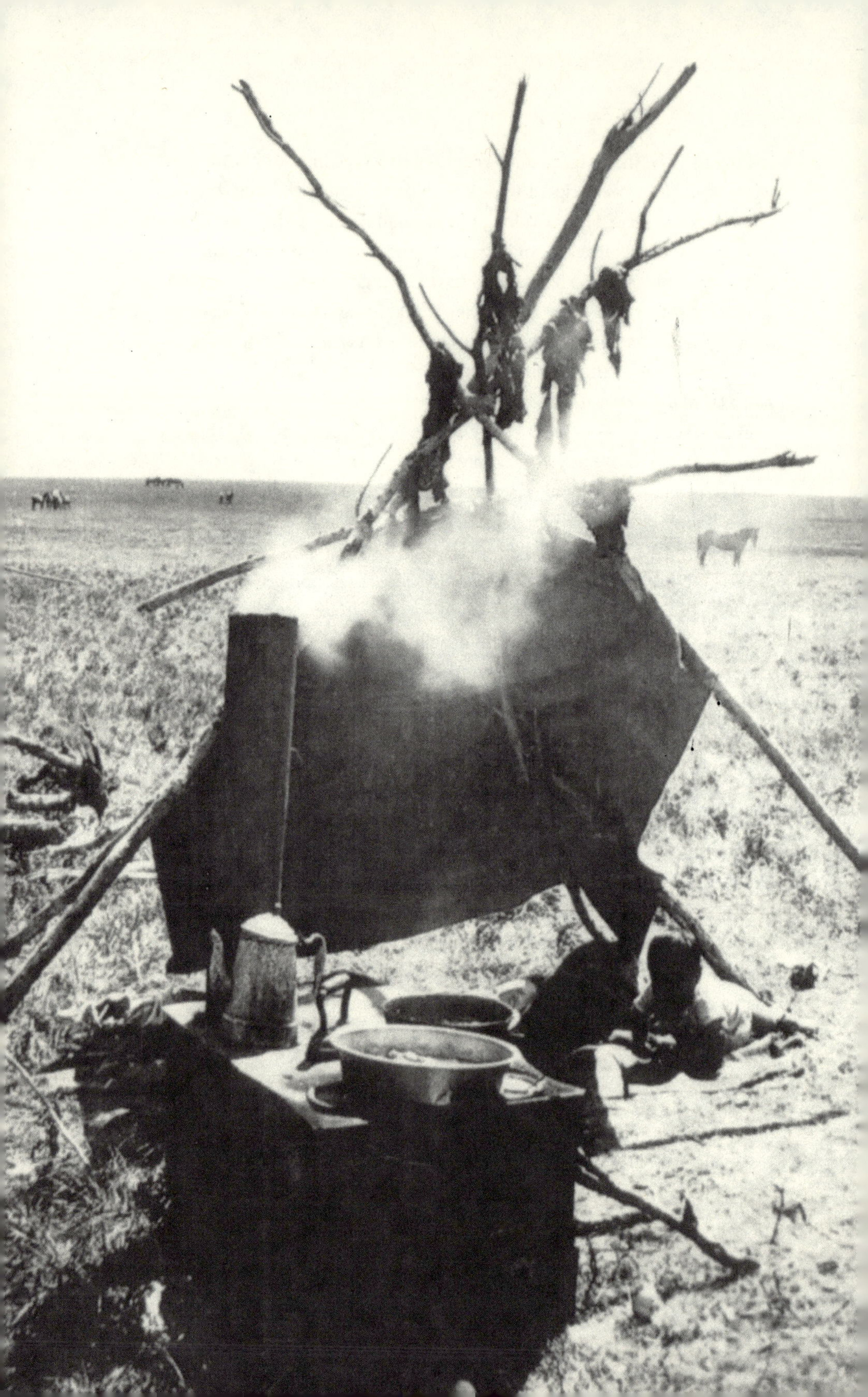

One

In the old days, they danced all night. A lot of people used to come—different tribes, different Indians.

Now, the Peigans used to travel all the way down to the Kootenays. We used to be able to ride on the Dayliner that used to run through the reserve. Everybody used to go up to Brocket on the passenger train to the place where the Dayliner would stop. Once the train got to Brocket, everybody spent the day before and slept at night at the station, waiting for the train with all their bundles of stuff that they're going to be travelling with. When the train came in the morning we all start loading up our stuff and a group of people would get in. We all headed out towards Cranbrook [British Columbia]. That's where we all go.

"Kootenays" denotes both a First Nations' people, now called Ktunaxa, and the mountainous region in southeastern British Columbia that is their home territory.

Trips to the Kootenays are recorded on Bull Plume's winter count: "All went to the Kootenay Indian Reserve on their first visit" (1907), and "When Indians went to Omaha and Kootenays" (1916) (Raczka, 1979: 85, 88). The originator of Bull Plume's winter count is unknown. Raczka writes that Iron Shirt, father of Brings Down the Sun, was probably the second keeper of this winter count. Bull Plume kept it for a time then gave it to the Anglican missionary Reverend W.R. Haynes and translated it for him. Haynes added entries to the winter count while it was in his possession 1912–1924 (Raczka, 1979; Brownstone, 1993). Bull Plume (c.1856–1920) was born Siksiká (Blackfoot) but was adopted by Piikáni (Peigan).

On opposite page: Making dry meat on the Peigan Reserve, c.1920s. Probably photographed by Peigan Indian Agent Chester Arthur. (Glenbow Archives, PA 3280-3)

Train depot at Cranbrook, before 1904. (Courtesy of Royal BC Museum, BC Archives, C-08272)

We all go visit the Kootenay people. They had nice horses. They'd decorate their horses up and they would put bells on their horses. When they're trotting along you could hear the bells jingling away. A lot of them had sleighs and teams and people would be in these sleighs. Those people all lived around Cranbrook. They would meet us all at the train station. They would take us to their different homes, especially the ones from Peigan. That's when I used to be there with my dad and my mother, when I was a little boy.

That's the time when they used to eat around, New Year's. Everybody would eat at different places. They looked after Christmas the same way. We'd come home with a lot of dry meat, buckskin, deer hides, and deer dry meat. That's when I first knew *omahkatoyi-iksistsiko* [big holy day, Christmas]. The Kootenay people had songs before they have big holy day, the night before, Christmas Eve. This is what we call a Christmas carol. ... [T]hey are Indian songs and they would sing all these songs. All the old people knew them back at that time. Here is one. [He sings a carol.] We all used to stand

Kootenays at Cranbrook train station, 1926. (Courtesy of Royal BC Museum, BC Archives, I-30604)

outside. My cousins and my relatives all know it well. I used to hear them sing that in the Kootenays and when we got home they always used to stand outside and sing that song and other songs, and they pray. They're the ones that brought me to survival when I was young. At those times I was told, "This is how we all treat each other and we bond our relationship as a group of people." That was how I knew life.

Well, I was given a present from the Kootenays. It was at the time of big holy day. I got a saddle blanket and a pair of furry chaps. When I got home I gave them away to one of my relatives. There's lots I want to talk about.

Now, these lodges, the one I'm sitting in now, this was my dad's home. The Snake design was my dad and my mother's lodge. And my other lodge, my other home, [is] the Elk design. Then my other home, [is] the Buffalo Hoof design. All the songs were sung to me and all the designs were transferred to me, I didn't take them for free. I made offerings and payments on them: goods, horse, and money.

Those people had good years. Now, governments are putting us in a different way. When we start living well with their governing, then they change the rules on us. Today, it's still like that. Now, young people today don't speak Blackfoot anymore. Their language is starting to be lost. That's why they don't hear us when we tell those things. It's a pitiful life. If they don't look after themselves, these young people, it's gonna be really pitiful the way they live their lives. That's the way I've been thinking about life now.

We used to go up to the Timber Limits [Peigan Reserve timber allotment] and chop wood for white people so that they could give us cattle. When we got cattle we had a good life. They used to give us eggs, beef, cows, and horses. The old people used to [go] up in the Timber Limits and cut trees and posts for those white farmers. That's when the old people said again, "You look after our forest up at the Timber Limits. Don't just wreck it." When the sawmill came in, they really wrecked the forest up there. Today, nobody goes up there to chop lumber any more. Chopping lumber is faster today. We've got chainsaws that cut wood, and we can knock trees down left and right. That's what the old people warned us about. They told us to watch our forest, "Don't just wreck it for nothing."

The Timber Limits is a parcel of land in the Porcupine Hills northwest of Brocket set out in Treaty 7 as a separate part of the relatively treeless Peigan Reserve so that Piikáni would have a free, renewable supply of timber. An early newspaper article, titled "The Dusky Indians, Their Advancement," reported: "About 1,700 logs and rails have been cut at their [Peigan Reserve] limits and hauled to their reserve for houses, stables, corrals and fences" (*Macleod Gazette*, 12 July 1895: 1).

Today's life is a lot different. Now, when I started farming here on the Peigan Reserve, I saw the steam plows, the steam tractors. Everybody got fifty acres plowed. Then people started farming their own. Everybody back then started trying hard, working hard. Young men, young women, and all our people, they all tried and worked hard. They had a lot of rich crops.

Óki. Now all our farms are leased out; they're all loaned to white people. The "before people" did all their own plowing and farming. The old people said, "The earth is heavy. If you're strong and young-willed, you'll be able to farm." When I was young, I really tried hard with my farming. I took just about all the land that was given to our family and plowed it all up. My dad gave me his farm land. I plowed and worked for him.

Peigan Indian sawmill in Porcupine Hills. Photographed by R.N. Wilson, 1892. (Glenbow Archives, NA 668-73)

The photographer, Robert Nathaniel Wilson (1863–1944), served in the NWMP at Fort Macleod and, beginning in 1884 and again in 1911, ran a trading post south of there near Stand Off. He was Peigan Indian agent (1898–1903) and Blood Indian agent (1904–1911). Wilson recorded ethnographic information about Blackfoot speakers, bought Native artifacts for various American museums, and wrote several scientific articles. Adolf Hungry Wolf reports he spoke Blackfoot and was known as Inuskaisto or Long-Faced Crow (1977: 20–21). "Most of his papers were destroyed shortly after his death by his executor" (Glenbow Archives, Robert Nathaniel Wilson fonds).

I went to school. When I finished school I went back to my father and mother and I worked hard for them. I was thinking about not having a pitiful life for my father and my mother: "Well, they're gonna feel good that I'm helping them. They're gonna find me useful, that I'm going to be working for them now." I worked for them. When my father quit farming, he said, "I'm going to give this land to you. I'm going to sign it over to you so that you can carry it on and live your life." Today my wife and my kids still live on that land. We have a good life. We lived a good, survival life on my land. We've got food, and we survived off of it. We've got hay and crops and exchange them for money. We found it useful the way my dad gave us his land for our survival. We made use of it to raise our children and family.

Also, I know there was a jail in town. Peigan had their own jail. The red coats [mounted policemen] stayed here on the reserve. They rode around, and, in later years, drove around in cars. They had a jail here and that's where they were able to put the boys, young people on the reserve who were getting into mischief, drinking, making mistakes by doing bad things. From that day the young people wisened up. They started to know the modern ways.

Plowing with horses, Brocket, Peigan Reserve, 1926; from the large Oblates of Mary Immaculate (OMI) photograph collection in Edmonton. (Provincial Archives of Alberta, OB 176)

"Red coats" refers to the scarlet serge uniform tunic worn by the North West Mounted Police (NWMP), formed by the Canadian government in 1873. The NWMP's red tunic readily identified them as Queen's soldiers (that is, British/Canadian) and not blue-jacketed American soldiers (Haydon 1971; Beahen and Horrall 1998). The NWMP evolved into the Royal North-West Mounted Police (RNWMP) in 1904 and became the modern Royal Canadian Mounted Police (RCMP) in 1919.

They also had a blacksmith shop. The young boys were taught how to work with metal, how to put shoes on horses, how to sharpen plows and haying knives, and all those different things. This guy by the name of Crow Flag, he really knew blacksmith ways. He was sent to blacksmith school. My father went to school in Calgary [St. Dunstan's Calgary Industrial School]. He told me stories. He said he had a hard time going any further in his education. So, hard work was what he was used to. He was taught hard work. He went up to grade five.

I'm not going to talk about the bad things that happened to me when I went to school. Those were part of my craziness too. I used to get whipped. I used to have hard times at school. When I quit school, I was taught farming ways, farm work. I used to work outside, working with horses and cows. That's why I was learning those ways. I found it useful to today. Then, years after, the Peigan people [elected] me as a leader, to become one of Chief and Council. I worked there for a long time. I really valued [or, safeguarded] my people [and worked] so that they would live a good life. That's when I knew that there was also bad life. I stopped the Peigan people from doing bad things to each other. [They should] honour and love each other. Today, it's really pitiful.

I worked for these churches on the reserve. *Óki*. I see the priests at church. They're needed people. They thought well of us and wanted us to have a good life. They looked after us at the time of death and prayer. The priests look after us right 'til we go back to earth. That I also took into consideration. Now, I also go to church, even if it's a white man that's priest. I remember all the sad, hard times when I'm sitting in church. I remember the old-timers, my friends and relatives, that have left us who we prayed for in this church and took out of this church with prayer. That's why I'm telling all you people, "Try hard. Pity each other. Honour each other."

Now, cows and horses. These white people that used to be bosses, that worked with livestock, they were good because we had a chance to thrive and expand our livestock industry here on the reserve. Our people had a good life with cows and horses, livestock. They all knew how to look after and herd them and put hay together, and everybody on the reserve used to all get together, families, to go out and cut hay. Then they used to take it down east to the place where we feed the cows in winter and stockpile the hay there [at the CY Band Ranch]. There was a lot of that, that I worked with back then.

Óki. All these people that had lots of cattle, we used to go work for them. White people, too. There was a man who lived across the river. His name was Red Wolf. He hired the boys from the reserve. His name was Maxwell. He hired Pards on the reserve. ... That's the time when he got hurt. Albert Pard got hurt from working with lots of horses. ... He suffered the rest of his life with hard life from these horses.

We went around having meals at different places, then in the afternoon the rodeo started. They had roping, had bronc riding, and they rode cows and bulls. Those were the ways we used to have rodeos and celebrations in the old days. We used to make our own corrals and arenas. There was a lot of lumber at our Timber Limits in those days. We used to just go up there and cut the posts and stuff we need to build fences. We'd all just tell each other, our friends and [me] putting up these rodeos, this is how many posts we have to bring down from our Timber Limits. We all worked for free. We put up our arenas and corrals together. Back then there were lots of cows and horses because we'd already rounded 'em up. On Friday, we'd already rounded up all the

One

The Old Man as layreader at old St. Cyprian's Anglican Church, Brocket, 12 March 1958. Photographed by Gordon Crighton. (Glenbow Archives, NB 44-58d)

Gordon Armstrong Crighton (1914–2000) operated a photography studio in Pincher Creek some time during the 1950s and 1960s. His photographs are in the collections of the Glenbow Archives and the Pincher Creek and District Historical Society (Glenbow Archives, Gordon Crighton fonds).

> Both Joe Crowshoe and Mike Swims Under (c.1914–1999) were related to Brings Down the Sun through their mothers; Mike's mother was Chases Back Alone. He died a week after the Old Man.
>
> The Sun Dance, or *Ookááń* (also *Okan*), is the most significant traditional religious event of the Blackfoot-speakers' year. Authority for putting up the complex Sun Dance comes through the *Naatoas* bundle.

animals and livestock, and we penned them up at the grounds for Saturday. Then on Saturday, we used them at the rodeo. The boys used to bring all their horses. There were a lot of horses in those days. White people used to come to these celebrations and see these horses and buy them — the buckin' horses. There were some that were really bad buckin' horses. They were bought by white people. They brought them to the States and up north to Calgary. They used them for bronc riding. They were wild. Back then the horses used to be really wild, more than today.

Óki. Just after they'd had a competition, the Indian agent all of a sudden came out and told us that it was too dangerous to have rodeos and ride livestock: "You're going to be taught how to play with a bat and ball and do different sports." So we had to start learning all these different things. We even had a team where all the boys started trying hard and they had a team called the Red Men. We became good at softball. There were others that ran foot races, ran long distance, and others used to high jump. They were good at that too.

Now, these things we're gonna write, I want to help people and other old-timers who know what I'm talking about. Our lives back then on the Peigan Reserve, and Peigan people, it was a good easy life to camp around. Today, all there is left from that life is only powwow and powwow competition. I'm getting up in age. I used to dance but not that much today. I really used to enjoy my powwow dancing days. Singing. I used to sing powwow dances for all kinds of people, all my friends. I made friends. Anybody who came to visit.

One

The Sun Dance is my grandparents, their Sun Dance artifacts and Sun Dance headdress my mother left with me. My partner, Mike Swims Under, we talk about it. We talk about how the young people today should learn these things and start bringing them back. Especially Sun Dance. But the rules that go with Sun Dance and ceremonies are really strong. If we can go the good right straight way in the Sun Dance, the way we used to have Sun Dance, it was an enjoyable good life. Since Mike and I are old people it's hard for us. We get tired. That's why we want to teach these young people our sacred way of life.

"[The Sun Dance] offered an umbrella for all kinds of other individual or group activities as the unifying ceremony ... The Holy Woman's sacrifice to the Sun, her vow made for the betterment of the tribal community and the insurance for its survival, the symbolic integration of the planetary constellation's importance into the ceremony are all factors that make the Natoas ceremony the central annual event in a Blackfoot tribe's cycle. ... [T]he Holy Woman's sacrifice with the help of the Sun Dance bundle can restore balance when there is a health problem, when there is a conflict between people themselves or people and the environment and when there is [or was] a lack of buffalo" (Crowshoe and Manneschmidt, 1997: 21).

Sun Dance circle-camp, Blackfoot Crossing, Blackfoot Reserve, c.1920s. (Glenbow Archives, NA 3331-1)

Now, these Thunder Medicine Pipe songs—Skunk, Larry Plume, these two people taught me. Larry Plume was a real knowledgeable man in Thunder Medicine Pipe practices and ways. He's the one that I follow today, his ways and teachings. I used to think about my father. I dreamt about him. I also dreamt about Bob Skunk a lot of times.

One

A STRONG WIND PICKS UP DURING THE AUDIOTAPING SESSION. RAIN PELTS LOUDLY AGAINST THE CANVAS TIPI COVER WHERE THE OLD MAN AND BRIAN SIT, SPEAKING ENGLISH, THE OLD MAN REPEATS WHAT HE HAD JUST SAID IN BLACKFOOT. THIS TRANSCRIPTION IS VERBATIM.

What the Bible [has], we have it in our Native way too. We have our prophets, too, in the Native way. I talk about the police work on the reserve. We had our own jail right in Brocket. Boys get caught drinking, misbehaviour. Some get thirty days, some get two weeks. I was a blacksmith beside the jail. I go and work there. And I go out and work for the old people: clean their yard, make a fence, help the old people.

I think [my] book [is] going to be very interesting. I don't want to say anything that will hurt the people, you know. Just like I'm telling reporters, you know. The other day I talked to the reporter. I told him, "The reporters and the Natives got to get together. Got to bring out the true issue of what the people want to learn." I'm all for these young people growing up. I want people to get some benefit out of the book, you know.

I spoke [in Blackfoot] about the changes of policies of the government. Once we were doing good. In those days we were doing really good, with farming and cattle and horses. We have milk cows, garden, everything. The Indian Affairs came and said, "You people got to get rid of your horses. We're going to bunch up your cattle in one place and you're going to feed them there." Changed their policy. That discouraged, confused, the Native people here in Brocket.

I started [a] boys' calf club and that was good. We won a lot of prizes with our calves. Oh, they're just Hereford, white-face calves, you know. They sold them in Pincher Creek. I told the boys, "Now, you boys have patience. Buy something useful." But a lot of them bought bicycles,

On opposite page: Mrs. Swims Under, Piegan, leading holy walk at a Sun Dance (in Montana?). No date. (Glenbow Archives, NA 3970-6)

baseball gloves [laughs]. I told one boy, he bought a calf. He bought a young calf. He had cattle ... when he grew up. And he told the boys, he told the 4-H calf club, "Joe told us to continue with the cattle." I worked with the district agriculturist, Ernst Steed, from Cardston. I get my grain and feed from the elevator. They have to write it down. After we sold those calves, we paid up everything. ... Then I started up Cadet Corps. I started Cadet Corps, be around about early part of 1940. I work with the Army barracks in Pincher. They supply all the uniforms and rifles. But they burned, you know, that hall, everything burned. Rifles and uniforms. All burned. ... [B]ig fire. One fella got burned in there. They were drinking in there.

We drove about six hundred head of horses here, right along here, taking them to Claresholm. My brother and me and two white fellas. Four of us. Took two days from Brocket to Claresholm. Corral them in the corral.

Nineteen-forty, 1941, '42, I was down in the States. I was working on Great Northern [Railway]. I get my free ticket and the passage anywhere I go on the line of Great Northern, you know. They stop at the station. I got a card. I go to the cafeteria. I want to eat. I just show them my card and they feed me. I don't have to pay for it [laughs].

I learned a lot about people. Different places I went: Mexico, Arizona, Los Angeles, down New Zealand, Australia, and China. I learned a lot about them. I keep my mind working all the time. Like in Calgary the other weekend [at the Calgary Stampede Indian Village], I put my chair outside. I sit. I sit outside and I see the people walking around. Looking at tipis, look inside. *Áa* [Yes], these people they want a lot more, you know. They want a lot more. Down in Virginia, Smithsonian, I was down there one month. We have a PA [public address] system in there. Sit inside. Talk. People, they come in. And they ask questions, you know, about all different things. Calgary should have one like that. Should have PA system. In the Indian camp, a lot of people come. Down in the Smithsonian they even record Indian song.

And we have college people come in. Oh, good. ... They like it, they like it. We put a plate here. They come in. They put money in there. In one hour I got about four hundred dollars. Fifty dollars, fifty-dollar bill, twenty dollars, ten-dollar bill. Hardly any change, you know. All paper money [laughs].

Two

TO THE GOBI DESERT

24 July 1992

RECORDED AT THE OLDMAN RIVER CULTURAL CENTRE, BROCKET, ALBERTA. ORIGINAL INTERVIEW IS A MIXTURE OF ENGLISH AND BLACKFOOT. REG CROWSHOE TRANSLATED THE BLACKFOOT ON 26 MARCH 1996.

JOE: As I was saying, Brian Noble is a stranger to me. I didn't know him at all until one day we had a camp down the river. ... have a Sun Dance, when Reggie and him came. Reggie told me, "This young man wants to see you." I told him, I told Reggie in my Blackfoot, "I don't know him. Where did he come from?" "In Edmonton." "What is his occupation?" "He's working with [Ex Terra's team of paleontologists] and right now they're planning they're gonna go to China and you are nominated to go with them. Brian Noble will tell you the purpose that you are going to China." So I told Brian, "Right now where I am with these camps here I'm occupied with ceremonials. I've got no time for you now. Come back and see me again." So he left.

After we broke up the camp I had another invitation down in Great Falls [Montana]. For another four days I was down there. ... Right after the breaking up the

Brian Noble co-founded Edmonton's Ex Terra Foundation in 1983 to organize and undertake a multi-year series of paleontological expeditions and cultural and educational programs in China and Canada.

camp we went down to Great Falls. We got involved with some of the millionaires down there, big ranchers. They gave me a horse that year. I had to do some work for them.

When I came back Brian came back to me. I told him, "I want to make you understand. I'm goin' to build a sweat lodge and you're gonna come in with me and then I will know if you are serious concerning about what you want to see me for." So, we got in a sweat lodge. And it was awful hot. It's a different heat than sauna. You go, you get in a hotel, you go to the sauna, it's a different heat. Right there he started to learn our Native way. He came out with me. He [had a] ... very honest way of tellin' me about the trip to China.

So I left here and I went to Calgary and then I flew from Calgary to Vancouver. Then from Vancouver we flew all night; eleven hours we travelled over the ocean. We got to a place where a lot of people got together, Tokyo. We stopped there. It was an expensive place. We went to eat at this place and there were a lot of short people there. There are a lot of them around Taber. They're Japanese. Then we got to China. There was this dance I went to when I was a young man and they gave me a name. They called me "Big Chinaman." And I thought when I was there, "Now I really took that name, Big Chinaman. I'm glad. It's good that I came to China."

The Canadian government forcibly evacuated more than 21,000 Japanese Canadians inland and away from British Columbia's Pacific coast during World War II. They were interned at three road-building camps, two POW camps, and five self-supporting camps across Canada. Some Japanese Canadians who chose to stay together as families were sent as labourers to sugar beet farms in the Lethbridge-Taber area in southern Alberta and settled there after the war (See W. Peter Ward in Nakano, 1980).

From there, when we got to China, we went another direction. We took those tipis with us. We already sent word ahead to get tipi poles for us. They brought us in another direction again in a plane. The Chinese people are really poor in the way they travel with their planes but we finally got to where we were going. We had a day rest there. The next day they took us out again. They brought us to the place they called the Gobi Desert. That's where the white people and some of the Chinese were digging dinosaurs. There were big dinosaurs they were digging. They were diggin' out their bones. It was poor, barren country.

We travelled all day in a vehicle overland. And then, finally, I got a chance to have my picture taken on a camel. I rode a camel. Then from there they brought us to another place, in the foothills. The people there were all on horseback. They rode on horseback. They came to a place where they met us. There were two horses there that I rode, one a white horse that they took a picture with.

We went through the Gobi Desert. We stayed there about four days. That was an awful place. One night it blew, the sand blew up. Oh, it was dusty. It wasn't high, it was low. Very fierce. I had one of these small camps [tents]. That camp can go up in the air. ... Some fellas came to [me], "Joe, you alright?" "Yeah, I'm alright." [laughs]. So I managed to survive that night. I got up in the morning and looked at my tipi. We had two set up. It was still up. Some Chinese had slept in there. I went over there. They're all gone, you know. During the wind they must of went out.

We had another trip going through Gobi Desert. Way up into the Mongolian Mountains. Going on that, on that journey, I saw some wild camels in the desert. I didn't know I was goin' to ride one of them.

Joe Crowshoe Sr. travelled to Xinjiang, China, in 1987 on a cultural exchange arranged by Ex Terra Foundation's Canada-China Dinosaur Project. Reg and his wife Rose returned to Inner Mongolia the following year. The Chinese later completed the Tipi-Yurt Exchange by presenting a yurt at Head-Smashed-In Buffalo Jump (personal communication, Brian Noble, 2007).

We had stopping places. There's lots of security in China. They have to ask you all kinds of questions. We go along for so many miles and then we hit a place where there's security and they had to stop, then we go and continue again. Along that journey we stopped in one place and I saw some, … out on the flat, funny looking tents [yurts]. I got one of them. It's in Edmonton. They look like a pup tent, but they're beautiful. Very beautiful inside. And I rode a camel there. I had my picture taken with it. Going on that journey up to the mountains, way in Mongolian mountains, and there I saw some riders. Mongolians had a bunch of horses. Awful small horses. We used to have them on the reserve here. We call them cayuses. Short wild horses, we used to have them here. I used to have one. And I saw them when I went over to that country over on the other side of the heavy water [ocean]. I rode two of them, a bay and a white.

The Old Man in Xinjiang, China, during the Ex Terra Tipi-Yurt Exchange, 1987. (Royal Tyrrell Museum/Alberta Tourism, Parks, Recreation, and Culture)

There were real bad bugs over in *Aapataamsstsinnimaa* [Chinese, "braids-in-back"], their land. There were … house bugs. White people call them cockroaches. Boy, are they ever fast! When it's dark, I could see them running around. When you put the light on, they're all gone. There were many [on] my pillow. I could see them running. And I tried to kill them. I can't do it. The next morning had to take my boots, scrub them using a brush, even my jackknife. I take them back to my home [laughter]. They told me next mornin', "Well, hi Joe, how you doin'?" I told them, "I was huntin' buffaloes all day, all night!" Not the kind of buffaloes we got here.

JOSEPHINE: No, we don't have them. We don't. Only Chinese people, the ones you went to visit, had them. I don't think we have them.

JOE: [China] was a lonesome place. … While I was sitting that night in my lodge by myself, I felt like I left my body. I was sitting back home in my own house back on the reserve. Then there was a knock at the door. Then I [was] brought back again. I'm walking around on the [Chinese people's] land. When I went back to my body I could still vision myself sitting in my own house next to the kitchen table. Then I knew there was a spiritual thing that happened.

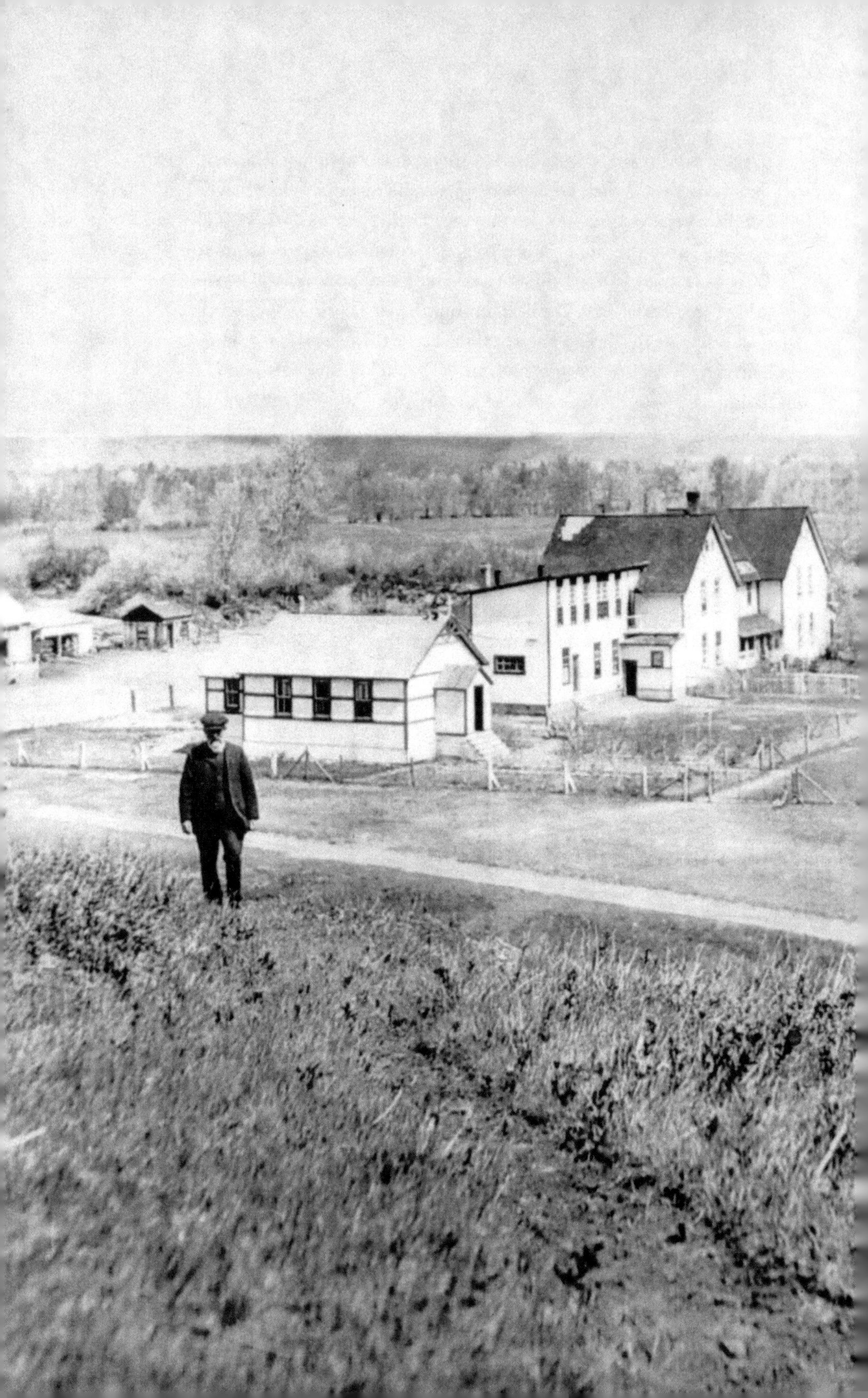

Three

BROCKET

18 October 1992

BRIAN NOBLE RECORDED THE FOLLOWING IN BLACKFOOT ON 18 OCTOBER 1992 AT THE CROWSHOE HOME IN BROCKET. BRIAN, THE OLD MAN, AND THE OLD LADY SAT AROUND THE KITCHEN TABLE. REG CROWSHOE TRANSLATED ON 26 MARCH 1996.

JOE: *Óki*. Now, this time I'm going to tell stories about my life and the way I know it and about the Peigan land. Back in the days when I was young I went to school up west [at Victoria Home Indian Residential School, two miles west of Brocket]. White holy people ran the school. I went to school there until 1928 when I left on June the thirtieth. I went back to my father and mother and I worked for them. I was helping my parents.

Óki. There was a lot of religious teaching when I went to school. Then there was a big flood in June 1923. The Oldman River flooded. It was a hard time, that time of the flood, because we were staying at the school. The bridge they used to bring the food and supplies across was washed away. … The river really flooded that time. That's when they took the school down and they brought them out to the new schools. They took the school down in 1926.

On opposite page: The Peigan Reserve Anglican mission and Victoria Jubilee Home Indian Residential School, 1913. It opened in 1898, was enlarged around 1900, and closed in 1926, reopening in Brocket as St. Cyprian's Anglican Residential School. (Glenbow Archives, NA 1020–23)

Fort Macleod in 1919, looking northeast. (Glenbow Archives, NA 3705-8)

Peigan children at the Anglican mission planting potatoes in spring, c.1900. Students at the mission's Victoria Jubilee Home laboured to help support the school. (Glenbow Archives, NA 1020-25)

I stayed back at the old school to look after the cows, horses, chickens, livestock. I stayed and looked after them for one month. A lot of mysterious things happened to me. I felt a presence in this big old house that I stayed in. I heard rattles. I saw ghosts. That was the old school and there were a lot of people that passed on there that probably came back and visited it the time I was there. I finally went to the new school when they moved out of the river bottom. I stayed there at the new school but I wasn't going to school at the time. I was just working around there doing the farming, the gardening, and then I left there.

Back in the old days, 1914, 1913, they were still operating the north white people [Hudson's Bay Company store] in Macleod. They used to make big boiling [soup] and people used to go there and buy in Fort Macleod. I used to go to Macleod with my father and my mother. When I went to school, the North West Mounted Police used to still be there in Fort Macleod. Then, when I left school, everything that I knew from that time changed. At that time, I thought I might as well become one of the priests, so I started working with the white holy men. That's where I started learning their white man religious ways. It was also a good way of life.

Óki. Me and my wife and my kids we learnt a good life from that. Then, around 1934, I lived with Far Away Nez Percé Woman [Pohkomaniitapatii]. Since then our family has grown with our children, our grandchildren, our great-grandchildren, our sons-in-law, our daughters-in-law. As time went on, I worked for my father in his farming. He gave me his farmland when I quit working with [the church]. He told me, "I'm gonna give you this farmland so that in the future you can make use of it for your own farming." I took it at that time. I tried hard on that land. I raised cows, pigs, and even chickens. My wife found it mysterious, even a miracle, how we survived. We had a hard time in our life. Now I'm getting older. I'm a real old man.

WEASEL TAIL

Now it's cold. This year [1992] it got cold really early. It was a lot harder in the old days when it got cold. ... Our people had to chop wood, make sure they hauled enough water, and that horses were looked after for feed. We learned to work hard because of horses.

My wife's relatives were all good, tough riders. I travelled with Bobby Warrior [Josephine's uncle] as he rodeoed around. He used to depend on me because I had to put the saddle on his bronc and I had to work with him in the chutes. I rode, too, and he looked after me.

Peigan students at St. Cyprian's Anglican Residential School, Brocket, 1947. Several of Joe and Josephine Crowshoe's children attended the new St. Cyprian's, which replaced the old Victoria Jubilee Home and was closed around 1962.

FRONT ROW, L. TO R.: unknown, Lewis Strikes With A Gun, unknown, Woodrow North Peigan, unknown, Arnold Crazy Boy, Wayne Knowlton, Allen Red Young Man, unknown. SECOND ROW: unknown, Rod North Peigan, George Crowshoe, Joe Crowshoe (Joe Jr.), unknown. THIRD ROW: Wilford North Peigan, Peter Yellow Horn, Jack Crowshoe Jr., Mervin Crowshoe, Jim Crow Flag, Tom Yellow Horn, Tyrone Potts, John Prairie Chicken. Fourth row: Albert Prairie Chicken, Harvey Yellow Face, unknown, Henry Potts, Robert North Peigan, Wilson Strikes With A Gun, John Weasel Bear, Gordon Morning Bull, and Melven Potts. (Glenbow Archives, NA 5508-3)

76

But I had a lot of injuries from riding broncs. Nowadays, as I get to old age, I'm starting to feel all those aches and pains from my bronc-riding days. We were people that rode horses, the wild broncs. We used to ride to different rodeos, and we used to ride a lot on the Peigan Reserve, out in the prairie. We had lot of horses. We used to have a big horse round-up and cow round-ups. It was our way of life. But today we live our lives very differently. Our young people are not strong people anymore. The old people were hard workers and strong. They had a strong will. Elders really helped us with their prayers. That made us strong-willed.

Josephine's uncle, Joe Warrior, competing in the Calgary Exhibition and Stampede, Calgary, Alberta, 9 July 1940. (Glenbow Archives, NA 3181-65)

When I left [school], there were a lot of different ways of making a living. [Our Peigan people] farmed and made money so that they could live a good life. We used to go and camp and rodeo in Lethbridge. We'd just leave our plows and stuff out in the prairie where our homestead was and go to Lethbridge for the rodeo. We'd come back and find things the same as when we left. That's how good the old people, the young people, and the Peigan people were. They never went around bothering other people's stuff or stealing from each other because they all lived a good life. There was no vandalism. They were smart in their ways. I always feel good when I get back to our homestead. Our equipment, the stuff we used to work with and our tools, were still where we left them. Nobody came to vandalize [our place]. Especially where we cut hay and made hay. People used to gather there to get hay. In the winter, they used to feed horses. We helped old-timers too. Any old-timers that didn't have hay, we would give them hay.

I also went south to the United States to work in the land of washing [Washington State]. I went down south on the train … I left my hay pasture, my wife with my tools, and all the stuff that I hay with. They put up the hay. She helped the old-timers too. We had enough hay that people came and we gave them hay. We helped all the young people and the old people. Me and my dad used to go hunting up in the Timber Limits. When we brought our game home, we gave rations out to the elders and the old-timers. People used to come to our place to visit and we used to ration out what we had hunted. It's very valuable that we help each other, that we understand each other as Peigan people.

Well, I hope young people today understand these things as our way of life. Deer Chief, my son Reg, and I, we are trying hard to show them these ways of going in right and straight directions so that they can start understanding the holy sacred ways and Creator's ways. Our Indian way of life was strong. My son, Deer Chief, and I, we want to bring our young people in the right, straight way so that our sacred ways will be stronger and better. Our Indian way of life was a strong and good way. That's the way things are.

Óki. Me and my wife live well. We're old people. We're getting up in age. In the old days, when I used to go out trapping, when I used to go out hunting, it was a hard way of life, not as easy as it is today. That was when I was young. During the cold days, we used to winter down along the Oldman River. Those were really cold, winter days. There were people that froze. I saw that. That I knew.

Óki. Now I've retired from that kind of life, the hard life. Now I'm just living here in the house. I get a chance to go around visiting in the States — Pendleton [Oregon], and where my son lives in Spokane [Washington]. Me and my wife go visiting. I take my wife to Nez Percé [Idaho] to see her people and her relatives. Today, we just use the telephone to go visit around, to see how we're doing. I'm warning you people today, "Try hard, help each other, care for each other, pity each other. Carry on and try hard in our sacred ways, our smudge, our prayers." That's the way it is.

PONOKÁÓMITAA: ELK=DOG

JOE: *Óki.* Now horses, the way I know them. … In the old days, our people, the old people, they called horses *ponokáómitaa*, elk-dog. The old people would say they're elk but they're also like dogs because you can ride them and use them for work. The people used the dog travois and used dogs quite a bit when they moved around. They hauled their stuff. They talked to them. Dogs and man understood each other in those days. Then the horse came along. When they saw the horse, they said at the time it was an elk. They said, "We're going to use them. They're 'elk-dogs.'" There was an Old Man that said the elk-dogs were saying, "I'm going to give up my body to Indian people so that they could use me and my body." The Old Man said, "Then I told the elk-dog, 'People are gonna be harsh on you. They're gonna whip you. They're gonna hit you in the face. Take pity on us. Don't hurt us.'" From there the saying came out, "Don't take things really hard if I said something bad to you because if you do it's going to hurt us both." We used elk-dogs quite a bit from that time. The old people used to go on conflicts and raids and horse races. The old people used horses quite a bit. There was also elk-dog medicine, what you use to cure horses that are sick or lame. There's medicine for horses.

Blackfoot-speakers (called Blackfeet in the US) first acquired horses from southern tribes around 1725. Ewers cites an early encounter recorded in David Thompson's *Narrative of his Explorations in Western America, 1784–1812:* "Soon thereafter, while hunting buffalo on the frontier of the Shoshoni Country, the Piegans [American spelling] encountered a lone mounted enemy. Although the rider got away, they managed to kill his horse with an arrow shot into his belly. The Piegans and their allies crowded around the fallen animal in admiration and wonder. It reminded them of a stag that had lost its horns. But as it was a slave to man they named it 'Big Dog.' Later the Blackfeet renamed this animal 'ponokomita' meaning 'elk dog,' in recognition of its size and its usefulness" (Ewers, 1958: 22).

Blood women and children with horse travois, Fort Macleod c.1890s. Steele and Company. Winnipeg, Manitoba. (Glenbow Archives, NA 006-1)

Three

THE OLD MAN RESUMES TALKING ABOUT HORSES IN ENGLISH. THE OLD LADY JOINS THE CONVERSATION. THE FOLLOWING IS VERBATIM.

JOE: *Óki.* And another thing ... the old people ... used to chase buffalo with elk-dogs. Not every horse. There're certain horses are really good for buffalo hunting, chasing buffalo. They're sure-footed. When horses came, ... the old Indians used to have a mare and a colt and they [halter-] break the mare. ... And they take them out and tie up the little horses, they tie them there, peg him there. Long rope. Sometimes colts they like to run around. They don't step in the holes, you know. They don't fall. And they know that's gonna be a good horse. Lot of the horses step in the badger hole and fall. They break their leg. But the old people train them to dodge the holes, you know. And a good buffalo horse chases the buffalo out on the prairie. They won't fall. ... [Horses have] a big head. They know it. They can size you up good. Sometimes I walk out here on the prairie with just my rope. When I seen my horses there, I walk up to them. Catch one of them. Ride them. Drive the other ones home.

JOSEPHINE: I'll tell you one story. When I was young [the Old Man] said, "My brother's gonna get the water for us." There's two horses there. And his brother went out there and these horses run away from ...

JOE: They're running away.

JOSEPHINE: [His brother] said, "I'm not gonna get water for you guys, because I can't catch those horses." I told him, "Where's that ... where's the bridle? I'll catch ..." So I just walked right up to them. They were standing there. I just walked right up to them! [laughs] I just walked right up! [laughing] Just walked right up to them. I put the halters on, I brought them, and [laughing harder] I brought them to Richard [the Old Man's younger brother] and told him, "Here's the horses. Go get us some water now." That's how horses are. They know people, if they know this person was gonna catch them. They know if he's kind to the horses, good to the horses, and let him catch them. But if they're afraid of somebody they'll run away. [That's] how horses are. I grew up with horses too. Really, I was! ... You know, you know, these stories are true! But *náápiikoan* [white man], you, you wouldn't believe it.

RATTLING HOOFS

JOE: My relatives tell a story about going on a war raid to a place in the south. I'll tell you a bit about it.

The people that they had a war with, the South People, saw them sitting in this valley. The one that saw our people in the valley went back to their own camps and told them, "Over here in this valley, there're some people sleeping there." Then those South People said, "Okay we're gonna gather up and have a war with them." These different people that came from the south, they had a war with the Peigans and the Peigans ran into the trees. They ran into a group of trees. There weren't that many trees. Then the south people that surrounded this group of trees said, "Let them stay in there. We'll surround it and we'll start the trees on fire. We'll be able to raid them where they're sitting."

The leader of the Peigans was an old man. That night, while they were all staying in these trees, the Old Man had a dream. He was told in his dream that the South People were going to burn them out, but the person in his dream told him he was going to save

> The identity of these "South People" is unknown. Alberta archaeologist Jack Brink has written about the complex geographical occupations of the northwestern Plains by tribal groups during the eighteenth and nineteenth centuries (Brink 1986).

them. He said, "In the morning there's gonna be fog and nobody's gonna be able to see anything. I've got some hoofs over there in my stuff. You're gonna hear them. Wherever you hear the hoofs rattle, just follow that sound. These people that surrounded you, that are planning to burn you out, your enemies, will not hear or see you." Well, the South People sat there and watched the bushes, watching the Peigans. They were making sure that nobody escaped that was in the middle of these bushes. In the morning they started the forest on fire and they burnt everything out. They burnt all the trees down and the grass but they didn't find anything.

The mysterious man that came in the Old Man's dream took all the Peigans out of this situation. The mysterious man told them, "I'm going to go through this valley and you're gonna be hearing these hoofs rattling. Just keep following. Nobody's going to see you." In the morning, the fog came in. They heard the rattle of buffalo hoofs and they started following. They came out of the valley and left. The rattling hoofs and this [mysterious man] brought the Peigans a long ways away. Then the fog lifted. This person told them, "You guys might as well start home. I've saved you from a dangerous situation." This is our traditional belief in prayers and in our true way of survival.

CENTRE-POLE TREE

JOE: *Óki.* Now, I'm thinking of the way I used to be back in those days. It was hard. I'm going to tell you something the old-timers told me a story about. Over here at Waterton, there were some elk. Today, there are always a lot of elk at Waterton. There was this man-elk there that was always getting jealous of the other elk. He always gets mad at the other elk. He told the female elk, "We're gonna go away. I don't trust you with the other elk. You're fooling around and playing with the male elks." They had a little baby elk, Elk Child. They went north.

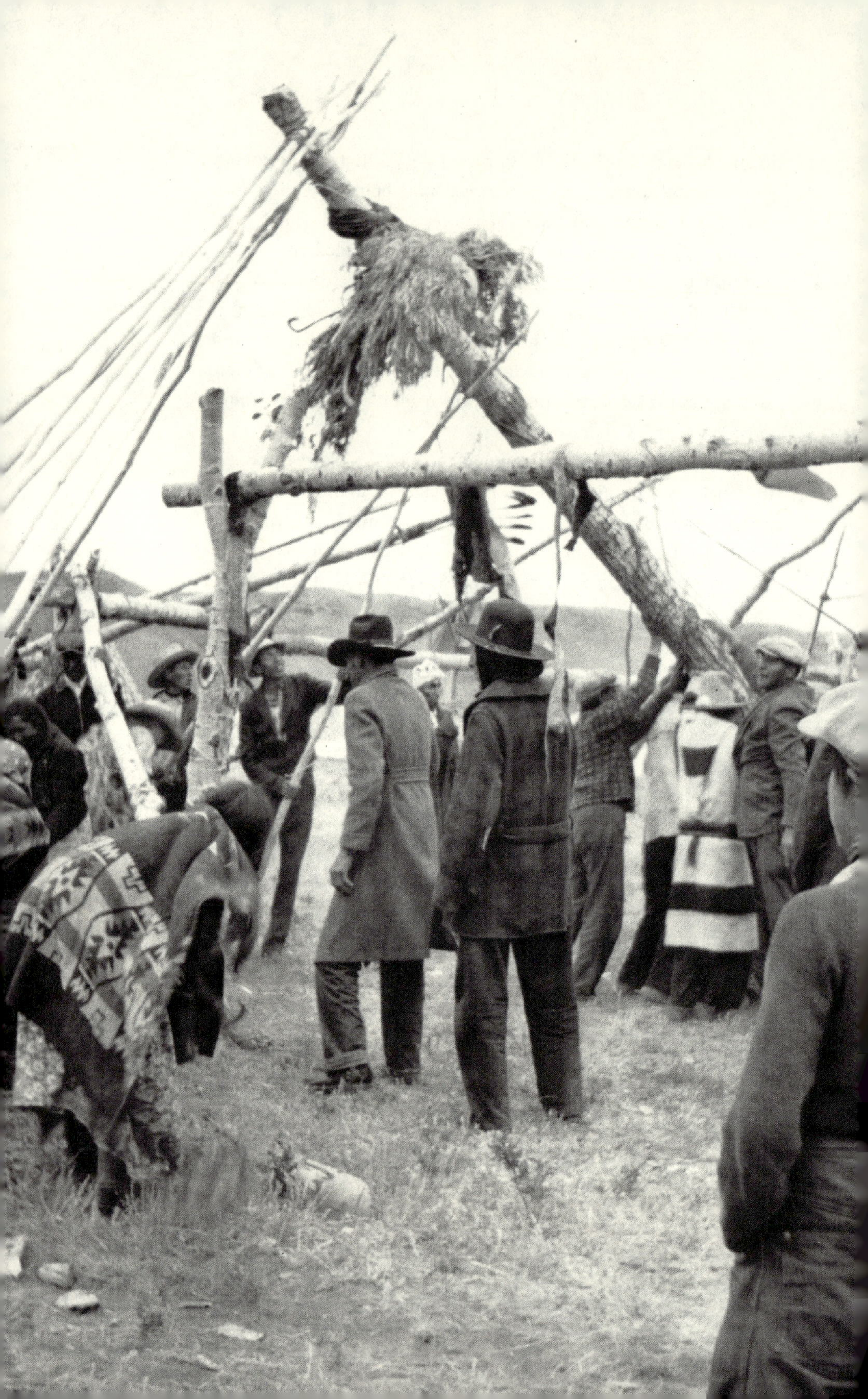

They followed the foothills of the mountains all the way north. They got to Red Elk River [Red Deer River] and stuck around that place. That's where they stayed.

Then he told his wife, "Now we're gonna have a confession. The biggest of all the trees here" (and this Old Man that told me this story said that one tree was a real big one and must still exist up there some place), the man-elk told his wife, "We're going to vow to this tree." The wife-elk told her man-elk, "You can go first. You go to the tree. If you can move it, you are right. If you can't move it, you are wrong." So the man-elk was there, getting ready. He went to the tree a number of times getting ready to move it. When he finally tried to move it, he couldn't do it. So he told his wife, "Go ahead, it's your turn now to move it." The female elk was getting ready. As she started, her hoofs were digging into the ground. Right away you knew she was telling the truth. She went up towards the tree four times and finally put her head against the tree. She almost knocked it over the way she shook it. This is her song when she walked up to the tree. [The Old Man sings the song.] She was making sounds at the tree. That tree is a Sun Dance centre-pole tree. The woman puts her head in the Sun Dance headdress and puts her head against this little tree in the Sun Dance lodge.

"Óki," the man-elk told her, "you've told the truth. You moved this tree and I know that you're saying the truth. You and I and our child are going to live a happy life. We're going to have a good life and I'm going to put away my jealousy. I won't get jealous of you." These stories are the stories we use to [teach] people about jealousy.

On opposite page: Raising the centre pole for the Sun Dance lodge, Blackfoot Reserve, near Gleichen, Alberta, 1938. (Glenbow Archives, NA-5452-44)

STOPPED IN A POWERFUL WAY

JOE: Over here at the Bloods there was this guy called [Rattlesnake] Calf Shirt. His son-in-law was a real gambler. He always lost. He was always losing everything. He had two kids. His daughter used to go back to her parents and tell them, "My husband has lost everything. Anything good that we have, he loses it, even his clothes, his wagon, harness; he bets them, he loses them." She said, "I'm coming home. I'm not going back." The Old Man [Calf Shirt] sat there and never said anything; he was just thinking. How is he going to deal with this situation that was bothering his daughter? His son-in-law's life and gambling ways weren't right. This was just happening; it hadn't been going on too long. The next time his daughter came back home again he knew his son-in-law had lost everything again. So he didn't give any more stuff to his daughter. She said they'd lost their saddles, their harnesses, their horses, all their good stuff.

Then his son-in-law suddenly came into his lodge. The Old Man told him, "Oh. Come on in. I welcome you. Sit over here." The Old Lady gave him something to eat. Then he told him, "*Óki*, I'm going to make you a deal." He knew right away that his son-in-law came in to get something so that he could go gambling and bring his wife and his kids home. He told him, "Now I'm going to make you a deal. Tomorrow you get up early and you come over. I've got a horse tied out on a stake next to my lodge. He's my best horse. You get on him and you ride east and go up towards the Sweetgrass Hills around Monarch [Alberta]. On the south side of Monarch, in the coulee, there are big rattlesnakes all over."

Well, in the morning, the son-in-law came, got the Old Man's horse and took off. His father-in-law told him, "You get there before sunrise. When the sun comes up all the snakes will start coming out of their holes. After you've looked at all of them, you're going to see a big one. It's a big snake. He's gonna come around you. He's gonna act like he's

Three

Rattlesnake Calf Shirt c. 1886. Photographed by F.A. Russell, Lethbridge, Alberta. (Glenbow Archives, NA 716-4)

gonna bite you. Here's some medicine. Put it in your mouth and just keep chewing it. And you kind of spit around you so that he won't attack you but will settle down around you. You pick him up and wrap him inside your shirt."

Well, the son-in-law felt that this was really dangerous. So he came to his father-in-law's the next morning, got on the horse, and went down, about ten miles down. He waited there. He tied his horse and waited. It was sandy country and rocky. When the sun came up, the rattlesnakes started coming out. He started looking. He thought, "That's not the one. That's not the one," as the snakes crawled out. Finally, one big one crawled out. When he crawled out of his hole, the son-in-law saw him right away. That big snake came up to him and started acting like he was going to bite him. It started to get after him. He knew, "This is the one, this is the one I have to take." So he took the medicine and he started biting on it. Chewing it. He did what the Old Man had said [spitting on his hand, gesturing towards the ground, as if putting his hand to a smudge, and gesturing towards the big snake], "Calf Shirt told me I'm supposed to come and get you. He wants you." Then the big snake settled down. The son-in-law said, "I've got to be brave. Oh, I've got to be brave." He took the snake and he tucked him into his shirt and he wrapped the snake around. The son-in-law was finding this far too dangerous and he was really scared. The big snake wrapped himself right around and he could feel him scraping against him. He walked to his horse and was finally able to get on it. He said, "As I travelled and started bouncing the horse, the snake started getting tighter around me." "Then I thought, 'I hope this snake doesn't do anything to me. I vow that if I get him to the Old Man and he doesn't do anything to me, I'm going to give up my gambling.'"

He took him home to the Old Man right away. He pulled up with his horse and told the Old Man inside, "Here it is." The Old Man inside said, "Bring him in." He got off his horse and went in. The Old Man had a black handkerchief spread out beside his bed. When he got in the house, he took him out, and right away the snake unwrapped himself from his son-in-law. The Old Man just covered the snake right in front of him with his black handkerchief. He told his son-in-law, "Right, now you can take your wife home."

The man took his wife and kids home. There was some firewood there. He took one stick of firewood and told his wife, "Take this wood and put it in the fire. That's my gambling. I'm gonna burn it and I'm not going to gamble anymore." The woman told him, "No. You said that you don't want to gamble anymore. You're the one that's gambling all the time, losing everything. You get up, take that stick, and put it in the fire." That's when the man knew, "My father-in-law warned me and stopped me in a powerful way. Right now I'm going to quit gambling. I'm going to put it away." And he quit all his hand games and gambling and then finally started building his wealth. He built up his wealth pretty fast. Soon he had three lodges. Inside, they were well equipped. Lots of food. So one day he told his wife, "Alright, invite your parents, your father and your mother, to come and visit." The girl went and told her father, "He wants to have a smoke with you and to eat with him." So they visited him.

The Old Man knew as he got there, he already knew ahead of it, this is how it is. "*Soka'pii* [good]. He took my word. He quit his gambling and has built up his wealth." They went over there and went into in his lodge. He thought, "Boy, they had nice things in their lodge!" His daughter fed him when he was there, gave him a few blankets as presents. Then the girl went out of the tipi and went into the next tipi and started making lunch again. And then the girl came back and told him, "This man next door invited you. When you finish go to the next tipi." The man went out and he went to the other lodge. When the Old Man and the Old Lady came, they were invited in again. It was his son-in-law that was sitting in there and that had invited them into the second lodge. Again, he fed them and gave them goods. Then he told them, "There's another lodge. You're invited again." So he walked out and went to the next lodge. When the Old Man and the Old Lady came out of the second lodge they walked to the third lodge and went in. The son-in-law was sitting in there again. Then the Old Man told his son-in-law, "Now your life and your ways are good. You're not gambling. Are all of these lodges yours?" And he said, "Yeah, they're my homes." And he said, "This last tipi you came in is yours. I give it to you. Here are my horses. Look at them, and any of them that you like you can take them." Hey. And that's when the son-in-law quit his gambling and he really had a good life after that.

These are the stories the old people told us to stop us drinking. The same way as in this story. Young people today don't listen. Now, hard methods were used to stop this man from his bad ways. He learned from those hard ways, from the snake, and from the Old Man's power. He respected them and he quit his gambling. From then on, he lived a good life.

Hugh Dempsey writes how Calf Shirt first gained his personal rattlesnake power (see this same article for another version of the Old Man's story): "According to elderly Bloods, Calf Shirt [1844–1901] received his rattlesnake powers through a vision in the late 1870s. The event occurred shortly after Calf Shirt's father died and the young warrior had wandered away by himself to mourn. The Bloods were camped in a rattlesnake-infested area east of the present Medicine Hat, at a place called 'Where We Drowned.' Calf Shirt walked aimlessly in his sorrow until, at last, he laid down exhausted on a sand hill and fell asleep. While there, he

---

On opposite page: Rides-at-the-Door (Blood), the Old Man's father's half-brother, photographed by W.D. Marsden, 16 January 1958. (Glenbow Archives, NA 1757-4)

From a series of photographs W.D. Marsden made on the Blood Reserve in January 1958 while working with Hugh Dempsey of Calgary's Glenbow Foundation. He also worked at Cluny on the Blackfoot Reserve on the unique 1961 film *Okan, Sun Dance of the Blackfoot* (Glenbow Archives, Okan: Blackfoot Sun Dance Film Project fonds, access restricted). Bill Marsden, was Alberta Film Commissioner from 1980 to 1993 (Bill Marsden to Mike Ross, personal communication, 2003).

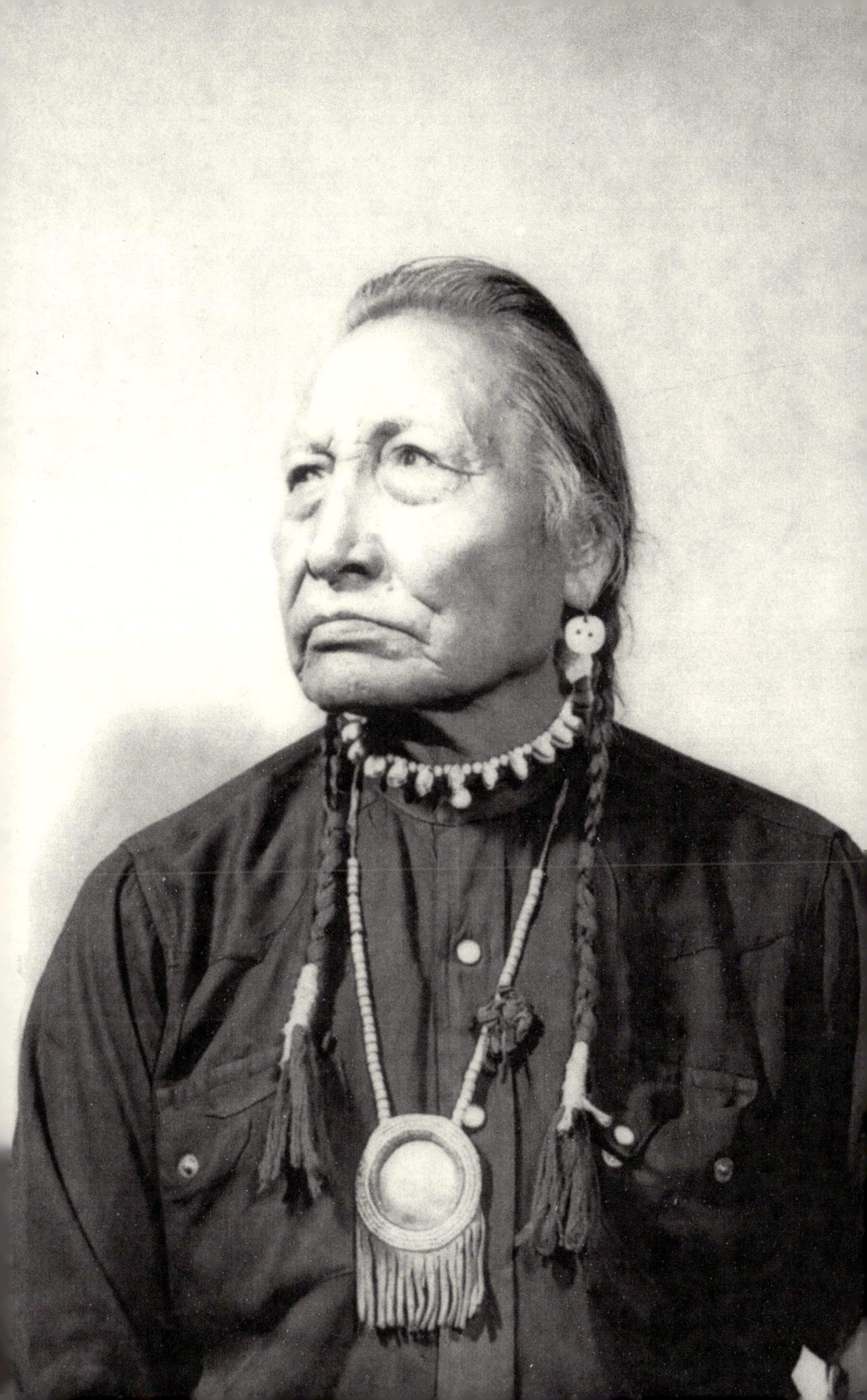

had a dream in which a person appeared before him. 'I've heard you mourning the loss of your father and have taken pity on you,' said the stranger. 'My father has sent me to you to say that you'll be his son and we'll be brothers. All of our people who live here are his children and you are now one of us. You'll become a leader of your people and we'll watch over you. Always carry some sage brush with you so that we'll know you and so that you can use it to treat those who are sick'" (*Alberta History* [1981] 21: 4, 2).

That was Calf Shirt's son-in-law. Blood Indians. Rides-at-the-Door was the one that told me the story. He's my relative [Joe Crowshoe's father's half-brother]. He told me a lot of stories. I just told you this story so that new people can guide themselves in the future. I hope these young people would understand and listen to old people. What they're told by the old people always comes true.

Today, I keep busy. People and my kids come and visit and take me and my wife out to eat. Tomorrow we're gonna be busy again. The Peigan people have asked me to pray for them. They're going to have a big meeting. Council and Chief came and invited me to go to say the prayer. I've always found these kind of things hard to do but I always try hard. I always think the best for people and want happiness for people. And that's the wise words from elders. We had these kind of things happen to us, me and my wife. These old people have been talking to us. I used to think, "Well, I'm not going to do this bad thing, I'm going to try hard again." Today I live a good life. I pity people and I enjoy people. My prayer is the most important thing to me. We bring ourselves in a good way, in a straight way. Creator hears us.

THE SHORT THUNDER MEDICINE PIPE

JOE: *Óki.* I was transferred the [Short] Thunder Medicine Pipe bundle. There was this Old Man that came to my house and told me to come and get him so he would live with us in our lives. That dream happened where they lived on the farmland my father gave me. So I went and I got my dad's Thunder Medicine Pipe bundle. ... Now we're old people. I raised my kids in a good life with it. I really looked after my Thunder Medicine Pipe bundle.

The Old Man described getting the Pipe in a 1997 interview with Sybille Manneschmidt: "Where I slept I had a dream of a person who came and said, 'Come and get me.' I dreamed the same dream the next night. That morning I saddled up my horse and told my mom. She said it was the Pipe talking and I should [go] and get it. The next morning I put up my horses and the buggy and drove up to my mother's house. She smudged and prayed with me and then we [went and] brought the pipe home. I have had the Pipe since then and take care of it" (Crowshoe and Manneschmidt, 2002: 70).

Now, there's a lot I want to talk about, of stories, old-timers. I gained wisdom from them. I wasn't smart right from the beginning. The old people were the ones that gave me knowledge and wisdom. They transferred to me their words, their wisdom, their songs, the way of life, and Sun Dance and Medicine Pipe ways. Now I'm to the point where I'm opening bundles. Larry Plume and Bob Skunk, Blood people, they helped me with these ways. They showed me these ways. They showed me in a good way. I find this kind of work useful to help our young people today. All these where you get payment from and goods and prayers, that's where I got help from. I always help people. I help people as best I can. I don't want them to live pitiful and hard. I was a leader. I was part of the council. I was one of the younger leaders. Pretty Rider, [Pat] Bad Eagle, those are some of the people I became leaders with. We all tried hard for the Peigan people to live a good life and give them a good life.

In the old days, the old people lived a happy life. They had happy times with their sacred ways and their celebrations, their dances and powwows, and even their white celebrations. At the time people

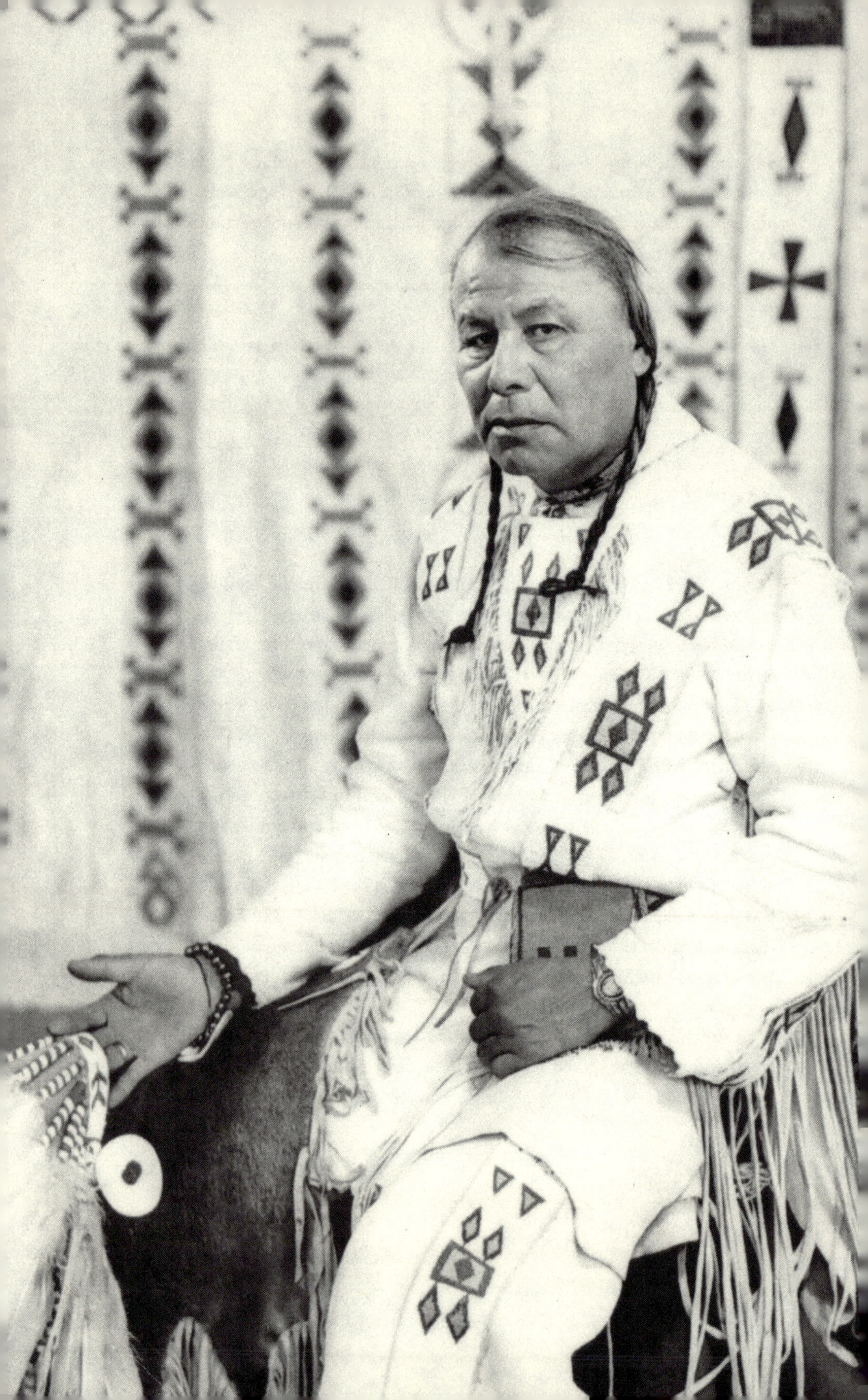

that do tricks [circus performers] even came to our celebrations. They came from Pincher [Creek]. People came from Pincher, Fort Macleod, to look at our celebrations and the circus. My father and my mother and myself, we used to go to them. But today, life is totally changed. That's because of school, education. Our young people are going in a different road. They're walking away from our traditional way of life. They don't care for the Indian way of life anymore. That's why I'm trying really hard, so that they can understand a smudge and our sacred ways. We had a good life and our Indian people had a good life. I'm not discrediting the churches, because I worked with them. They are the same and as strong as Indian religions. They gave us a good life. If we use our beliefs we live a good life.

Sweetgrass (*Hierochloe odorata*) is commonly used for smudging. It grows in low meadows and along road ditches in southern Alberta and Montana. Gathered bunches of its tall stems are made into braids about two fingers thick: "Small pieces [are] broken from the braid and placed on the hot coals. ... Prayers accompan[y] every smudge. It [is] believed that a person [will] not lie if he [uses] the incense." Some sacred items and ceremonies require smoke from sweet pine, or alpine fir needles (*Abies lasiocarpa*), as incense (Hellson and Gadd, 1974: 9).

Now today, my Thunder Medicine Pipe bundle was transferred to us in the proper way. Me and my wife we paid a lot of offering and payment on them, a lot of offerings and payment, horses and goods. Now we've lived to an old age with this Pipe. I'm really attached to my Pipe and I love and believe in my Pipe and way of life. I enjoy the Thunder Medicine Pipe Society ways. I go to Thunder Medicine Pipe dances in the States, in Browning and Bloods and different places where they have Thunder Medicine Pipe dances. I really find happiness there and I always like to go to them.

On opposite page: Pat Bad Eagle. Photographed by Gordon Crighton. 1958. (Glenbow Archives, NB 44-66a)

Lineage of Short Thunder Medicine Pipe Bundle

1. Made by Sooie (Charlie Reevis), Blackfeet, in Browning, Montana
2. Transferred to Fish Wolf Robe (Mamii'owa?), Browning
3. Given to Good Chaser, Blackfoot, in Gleichen, Alberta
4. Transferred to Hind Bull, Blood
5. Transferred to Many Chiefs, Peigan, in Brocket, Alberta
6. Transferred to Nathan Many Feathers, Peigan, Brocket
7. Transferred to Willie Crow Shoes (Awakasina), Peigan, Brocket
8. Transferred to Joe Crowshoe (Aapohsoy'yiis), Peigan, in Brocket
9. Transferred to Reg Crowshoe (Awakasina), Peigan, in Brocket

SUN DANCE VOW

A photograph in Beverly Hungry Wolf's *The Ways of My Grandmothers* shows Josephine Crowshoe's 1977 initiation as Holy Woman. The group also includes the Old Man, Mike Swims Under, and Mrs. Rides-at-the-Door, who was transferring the *Naatoas* headdress (Hungry Wolf, 1982: 178 [unpaginated]).

JOE: Small Girl, my daughter [Evelyn], came and told me she had had a dream. There was this person coming towards her telling her, "Your father and mother are coming, walking this way. Go and tell them to have a Sun Dance." I didn't really care about that dream. I came home. It must have been three years after and I told her dream to the Peigan people. The Peigan people told me then to go ahead and have a Sun Dance. It was a hard way at the time, the way we had Sun Dance. We were stalling and having a hard time getting going. Our old people were there at the time. They told us how to put together and start the Sun Dance again. We were trying all different ways. I was finally able to have my Sun Dance in 1977. That's when we had the Sun Dance again.

Mike Swims Under was the one that worked for us. There were a lot of people from the Bloods that came to that Sun Dance: Pat Weaselhead and Larry Plume and Chief Calf. My mother was still alive that time. My daughter, Evelyn, came to that Sun Dance and she witnessed her dream becoming a reality. From that time she started trying hard in her traditional ways again. This way of living our traditional beliefs is a hard life.

As time went on, I remember all the Sun Dances that have happened. Before these Sun Dances, at the earlier Sun Dances on the reserve, I had to work for the Old People. I'd go and chop the centre pole. The Brave Dogs had transfer. I was transferred at the time, and my wife was transferred also. Around those times before the '77 Sun Dance, our sacred ways and ceremonies started stopping. As time went on there were no more Sun Dances. My Sun Dance headdress was sold for me. It was sent to the Big House [Edmonton]. I finally got it back. I borrowed it, and then Wolf Fighter [Teddy Bastein] and [his wife] Holy Fox Woman had a Sun Dance with it. They had their Sun Dance lodge across the [Oldman] river.

Josephine and Joe Crowshoe as the newly initiated Holy couple, 1977. (Courtesy Royal Alberta Museum)

PARTIAL CROWSHOE FAMILY TREE

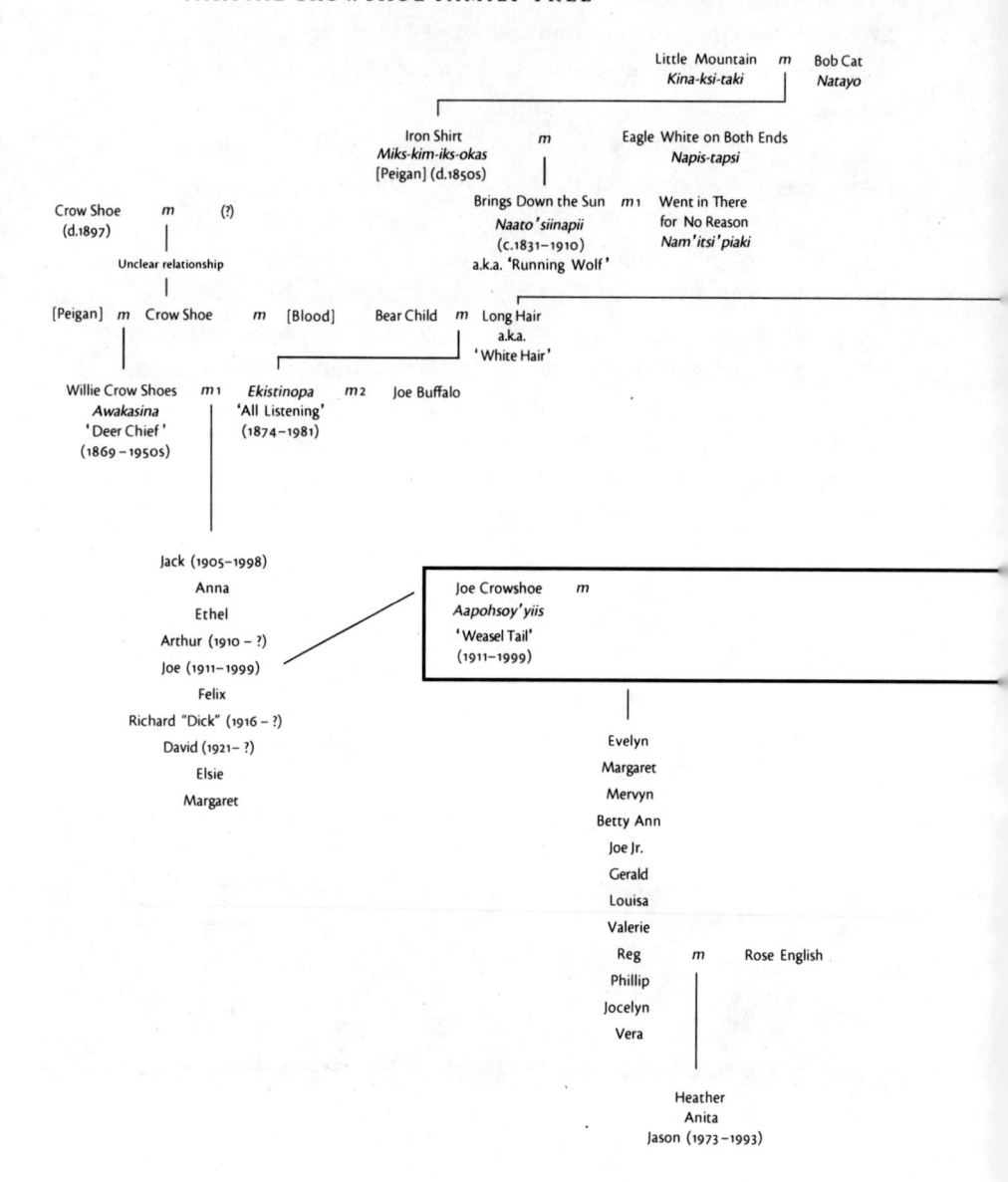

Little Mountain   *m*   Bob Cat
Kina-ksi-taki   *Natayo*

Iron Shirt   *m*   Eagle White on Both Ends
Miks-kim-iks-okas   *Napis-tapsi*
[Peigan] (d.1850s)

Crow Shoe   *m*   (?)   Brings Down the Sun   *m1*   Went in There
(d.1897)   *Naato'siinapii*   for No Reason
          Unclear relationship   (c.1831–1910)   *Nam'itsi'piaki*
                                   a.k.a. **'Running Wolf'**

[Peigan]   *m*   Crow Shoe   *m*   [Blood]   Bear Child   *m*   Long Hair
                                                               a.k.a.
                                                             'White Hair'

Willie Crow Shoes   *m1*   *Ekistinopa*   *m2*   Joe Buffalo
Awakasina   'All Listening'
'Deer Chief'   (1874–1981)
(1869–1950s)

Jack (1905–1998)
Anna
Ethel   Joe Crowshoe   *m*
Arthur (1910 – ?)   *Aapohsoy'yiis*
Joe (1911–1999)   'Weasel Tail'
Felix   (1911–1999)
Richard "Dick" (1916 – ?)
David (1921– ?)
Elsie
Margaret

                                      Evelyn
                                      Margaret
                                      Mervyn
                                      Betty Ann
                                      Joe Jr.
                                      Gerald
                                      Louisa
                                      Valerie
                                      Reg   *m*   Rose English
                                      Phillip
                                      Jocelyn
                                      Vera

                                             Heather
                                            Anita
                                      Jason (1973–1993)

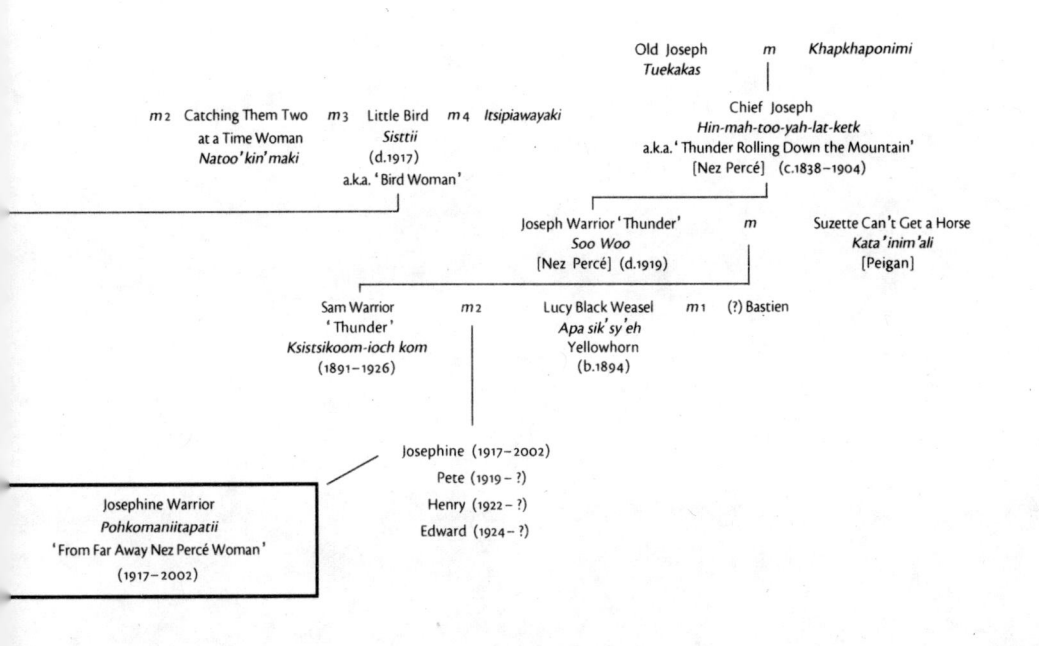

```
                                                    Old Joseph        m      Khapkhaponimi
                                                     Tuekakas         |
                                                                      |
                                                              Chief Joseph
  m2  Catching Them Two   m3  Little Bird  m4  Itsipiawayaki  Hin-mah-too-yah-lat-ketk
       at a Time Woman         Sisttii                        a.k.a. 'Thunder Rolling Down the Mountain'
       Natoo'kin'maki          (d.1917)                       [Nez Percé]  (c.1838–1904)
                               a.k.a. 'Bird Woman'
                                                |
                                    Joseph Warrior 'Thunder'      m      Suzette Can't Get a Horse
                                          Soo Woo                         Kata'inim'ali
                                    [Nez Percé] (d.1919)                  [Peigan]
                                                |
              Sam Warrior          m2      Lucy Black Weasel     m1   (?) Bastien
               'Thunder'                    Apa sik' sy'eh
           Ksistsikoom-ioch kom              Yellowhorn
              (1891–1926)                    (b.1894)
                                  |
                      Josephine (1917–2002)
                      Pete       (1919– ?)
                      Henry      (1922– ?)
   Josephine Warrior  Edward     (1924– ?)
     Pohkomaniitapatii
  'From Far Away Nez Percé Woman'
        (1917–2002)
```

*Information from: Peigan Reserve ration and treaty payment lists; McClintock 1968; Razcka 1979; David Thomas and Karin Ronnefeld 1982; Waldman 1990; newspaper obituaries; Oldman River Cultural Centre and pers. comms. Reg Crowshoe and Sybille Manneschmidt.

Four

ℬROCKET

7 February 1996

PROGRESS IN WRITING THE OLD MAN'S BOOK STOPPED FOR ABOUT FIVE YEARS. I KNEW EVERYONE INVOLVED AND WAS ASKED TO HELP. WE BEGAN AUDIOTAPING AT THE CROWSHOE HOME IN BROCKET ON 7 FEBRUARY 1996. NONE OF THE EARLIER TAPES HAD BEEN TRANSLATED, AND I DID NOT KNOW WHAT THE OLD MAN HAD SAID BEFORE. THEIR SON REG CROWSHOE TRANSLATED MY FIRST QUESTIONS FROM ENGLISH INTO BLACKFOOT, THEN TRANSLATED THE OLD MAN'S ANSWERS BACK INTO ENGLISH. BACK-AND-FORTH SIMULTANEOUS TRANSLATION FOR MY BENEFIT MADE DIRECT CONVERSATION AWKWARD AND WAS ABANDONED. THE TAPE WAS EVENTUALLY TRANSLATED BY JIMMY STRIKES WITH A GUN IN LETHBRIDGE. IN DECEMBER 1999, LEO PARD, A SON-IN-LAW, WAS ALSO PRESENT. MY FIRST QUESTIONS WERE ABOUT FAMILY HISTORY.

MIKE: **Where was the Old Man born?**

REG: **He said he was born at Wolf Flats. It's east of CY [Peigan Band Ranch]. That's where he was born.**

MIKE: **Who were his parents?**

REG: **His father's name was Deer Chief (Awakasina), [Willie] Crow Shoe[s], and mother's name was Everybody Listens To [the Thunder]. His [paternal] grandfather was Crow Shoe and his [maternal] grandmother was Long Hair.**

Ekistinopa, All Listening or Everybody Listens to the Thunder, was born c.1886 (according to the 1923 treaty payment list in Glenbow Archives), or in 1877 (*Lethbridge Herald* obituary). Her mother was Brings Down the Sun's daughter, Long Hair (also named White Hair); her father was Bear Child. After her first husband Willie Crowshoes died, she married Joe Buffalo and took the name Laura Annie Buffalo: "Throughout her life [Ekistinopa] was actively involved in the Sacred rituals and social functions of the Blackfoot culture such as the Sun Dance. She had assisted her mother [Long Hair] in ... 13 Sun Dances and witnessed many more after that on the North and South Peigan Reserves. She was initiated twice into the Horn Society and three times into the Brave Dog Society. Mrs. Buffalo was a previous owner of the Shortpipe Medicine Bundle which she passed on to her son Joe Crowshoe, but she continued to attend and support Medicine Pipe Dances on the North Peigan, Blood and South Peigan Reserves. Mrs. Buffalo was a strong supporter of all cultural activities and believed in preserving the Blackfoot language and culture" (*Lethbridge Herald*, 26 January 1981).

REG: **Deer Chief's mother [the Old Man's paternal grandmother] was from the Blood Reserve. Deer Chief's half-brother's name was Rides-at-the-Door. In the past the men had many wives. At the time, Crow Shoe had six wives. His mother's grandfather was Brings Down the Sun. Brings Down the Sun's wife's name was Bird Woman. Everybody Listens To's mother was Long Hair, who was a daughter of Brings Down the Sun. Brings Down the Sun's other daughter's name was Naatoyinaimsskaaii.**

MIKE: **What were your parents doing around the CY [Band] Ranch area? ... What did they do for a living?**

JOSEPHINE: **[Speaking English] At that time they don't work ... do for a living. They kill deer meat or whatever. They dried for the winter and they dig roots for winter. They live on their own. They don't live for money.**

Four

The Old Man's maternal great-grandparents were Brings Down the Sun (Naato'siinapii) and Bird Woman (Sisttsi). His weasel tail shirt and her *Naatoas* (Sun Dance) headdress are sacred regalia customarily worn on separate occasions. Photographed in 1905 by Walter McClintock at their camp in the Oldman River valley. (Yale Collection of Western Americana, Beinecke Rare Book and Manuscript Library, negative #39002037297166)

"[P]olygamy was common among the Blackfeet because it was a practical means of caring for the excess of women created by heavy war losses. ... Possession of several wives was one of the leading marks of the successful man. A few of the leading chiefs had ten or more wives. Probably at least half the men had at least two" (Ewers, 1958: 99–100).

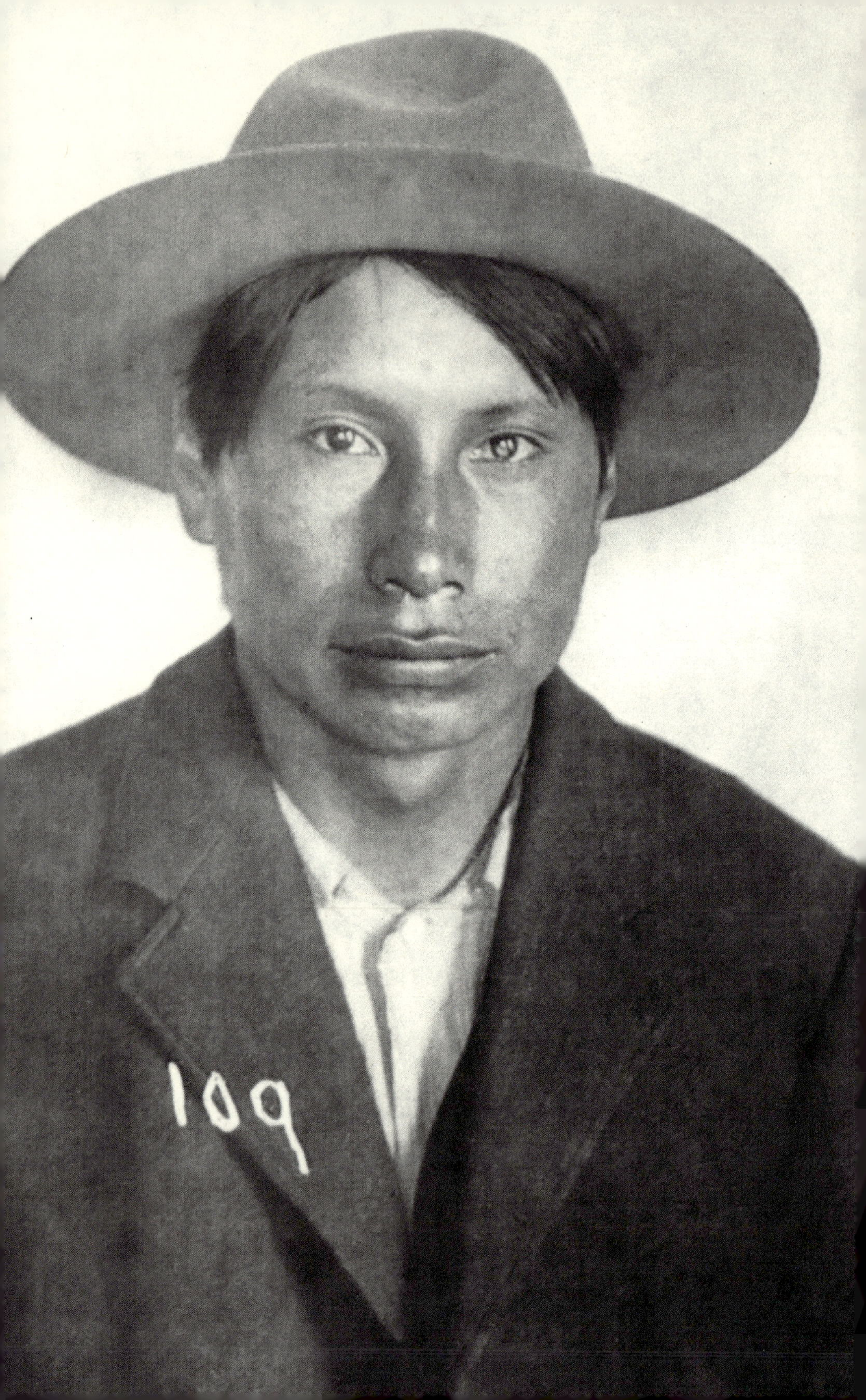
109

Four

Livestock crimes were common in southern Alberta in the 1890s and 1900s: "The Royal North-West Mounted Police at Fort Macleod dealt with 20 cases of horse stealing between December 1905 and October 1906, including Crow Shoes" (Beahan and Horral, 1998: 316–18). The 1907 RNWMP "D" Division Annual Report mentions Crow Shoes's trial: "At this court four Indian boys, named Philip Hoof, 'Yellow Creek,' 'Charlie Davis,' and 'Willie Crow Shoes,' were all convicted of horse-stealing, and sentenced, respectively to four[,] three, two and three years in the Edmonton Penitentiary. This slide-out horse-stealing case was very much on a par with the Fishburn horse-stealing case of two years ago. These Indian boys picked up horses of ranchers quite close to the reserve, and then ran them off about 30 miles to the north, and sold them at a ridiculously cheap figure to some farmers lately arrived in the country from the United States" (Sessional Papers, Royal North-West Mounted Police, Sessional Paper No. 28, 1907: 52–53). Willie Crow Shoes was out of the penitentiary and working for the Peigan Indian agent by July 1908 (Glenbow Archives, Indian Agency fonds M1832 f.6). Also see Dempsey (1995: 84–103) for a discussion of early cattle rustling and horse thieving, including Crow Shoes's case.

JOE: [In Blackfoot] They lived east of CY Ranch called Wolf Flats where they had their camp. There was no work at the time. Their survival was hunting and picking berries. Where [we] lived was Lone Fighter territory.

I remember when I was growing up at Wolf Flats in the summertime, we would go to Fort Macleod to get our treaty money. When I was young, we used to go to Cranbrook. We'd go by train. My father and I would go hunting in the mountains. We would hunt deer and elk and bring the meat home for the family. The reason why we went

On opposite page: The Old Man's father, Willie Crow Shoes, age twenty-five, in a North West Mounted Police photograph taken at Fort Macleod, 11 August 1906. He had been arrested for horse stealing. (Glenbow Archives. NA 258-7)

to Cranbrook and Tobacco Plains was to trade cloth and deer hide at Christmastime and New Year's. The Kootenay made good dry meat. Before the train, the people would ride on horseback to the Kootenay. That's in Cranbrook and Tobacco Plains. It would take them four days. They would hunt and fish.

Arni Brownstone notes, "After his days as a warrior ended, Running Wolf devoted his attentions to the religious and healing aspects of Blackfoot life (Brownstone cites Raczka, 1992: 68). This shift was marked by his receiving a new name, Brings Down the Sun" (Brownstone, 1993: 68).

'VISION QUEST

JOE: **Brings Down the Sun went to sleep on the hills to gain some wisdom. The holy spirits were coming to him to scare him. It was called his vision quest. The Sun told him, "[I'll] give you something that is very strong." Then the spirits really bothered him. He couldn't sleep. "I'm going to go home," he thought. That night [he] saw the sun. The morning after his vision quest he went back home and told the people, "I'm going to make the sun dance." He faced the sun, sang the song, the same song stopped it from raining, that same song, and made the sun dance. The sun was just moving. [The Old Man sings the song.]**

Edmund Morris noted Running Wolf in his 1907 journal:
"I also paint old Running Wolf, the oldest Peigan on the reserve. He is 83 years. ... Running Wolf came with gorgeous coat covered with ermine skin & his face painted yellow & band of hair attached to his own. The old man is anxious to have his eldest son succeed him as chief. This is now in the hands of the government. He spends his time now catching eagles in the mountains. His camp is 3 miles distant — about 6 lodges [house] his numerous kin. In his lodge he had the ——— of eagles arranged on an altar — hung sweet grass, a row of buffalo stones at the back, & rows of eagle feathers in a ——— cleared spot" (long lines denote illegible words in original diary; Fitz-Gibbon, 1985: 48).

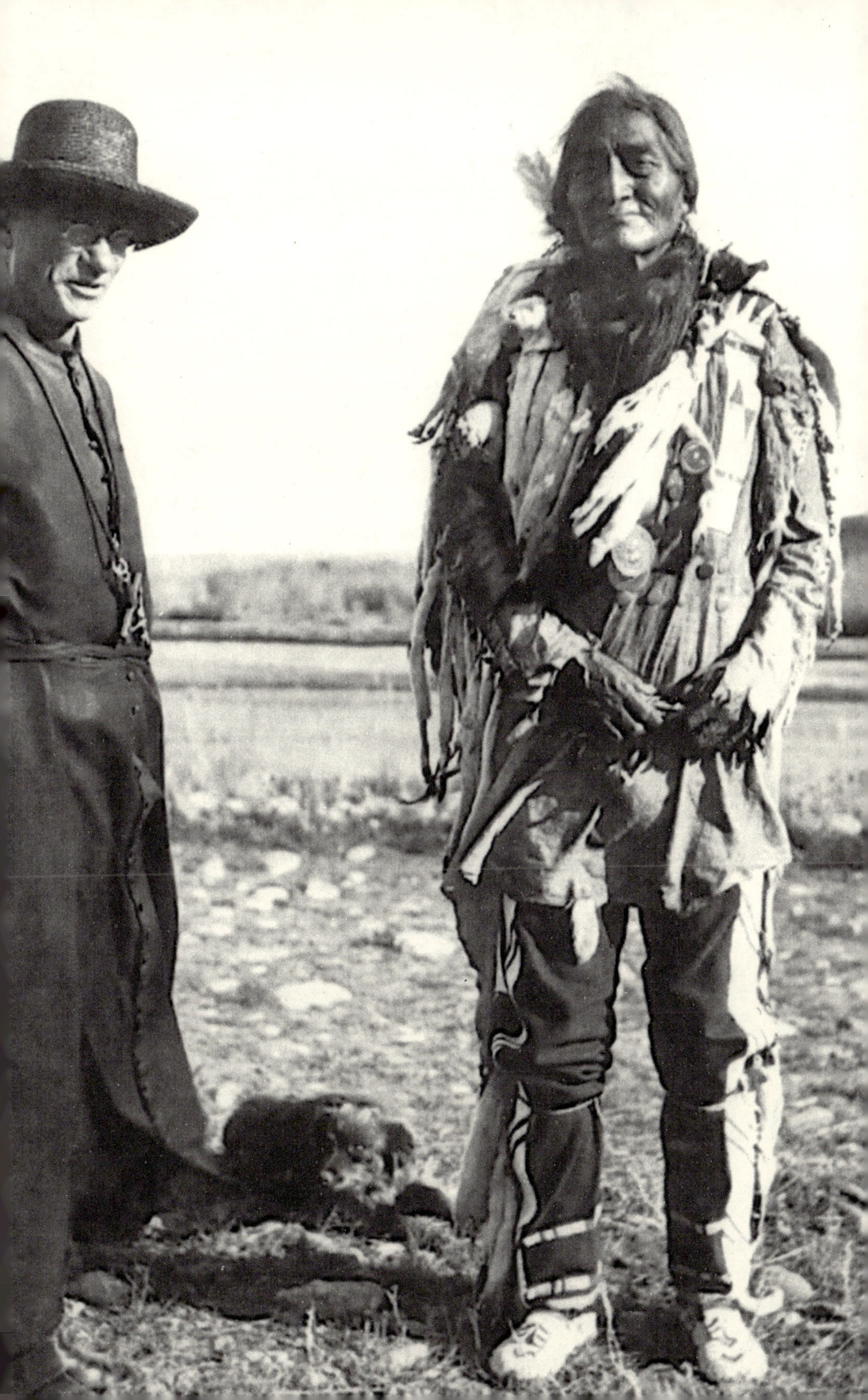

On previous page: Brings Down the Sun (Running Wolf) and Oblate missionary Father Léon Doucet. Photographed by Edmund Morris, Brocket, 1907. (Edmund Morris 18 [N13570], Provincial Archives of Manitoba)

Léon Doucet OMI spent over sixty years as a missionary among the Blackfoot, Peigan, and Blood people. The Oblates of Mary Immaculate (OMI) religious order were responsible for all Catholic missions west of Lake Superior. The Oblates established a mission on the Peigan Reserve in 1881 and operated Roman Catholic Sacred Heart Residential School there. Artist Edmund Morris, who met Doucet in 1907, noted he spoke Blackfoot and was called Little Father in that language (Fitz-Gibbon, 1985: 121). Father Doucet was born in France in 1847, retired in 1938, and died in 1942.

JOSEPHINE: [In English] That's true. I heard that many years ago.

JOE: [In Blackfoot] Brings Down the Sun was asked to stop the rain. It had been raining for days. They went across the river to the Sun Dance encampment, and they saw the rain coming. Black clouds. It was just black. So, they went and asked Brings Down the Sun if he could prevent it from raining. He asked them to make some fry bread and coffee. So, after he was done eating his fry bread and drinking his coffee, he took a feather and his robe. He sang a song and showed his colleagues how to sing the song. While he was singing this song there was a white man who witnessed it. His name was Pete LaGrandeur. He was the livestock manager for Peigan. He found Brings Down the Sun crazy. Brings Down the Sun was singing the song and holding the feather towards the cloud. But as he was singing, the cloud separated and it didn't rain.

Pete LaGrandeur (1890–1957) was a well-known Pincher Creek area cowboy, stockman, and rodeo competitor. His parents homesteaded just northwest of Brocket at the confluence of Pincher Creek and the Oldman River, later known as LaGrandeur's Crossing, where they built a stopping place for stage coaches. At thirty-four, Pete became Calgary Stampede saddle bronc champion and Canadian All Around Cowboy. He worked for various cow and horse ranches, as stockman for the Castle River Cattle Association (1933–43) and the Peigan Reserve (1943–57). He was inducted into the Canadian Rodeo Hall of Fame (*Pincher Creek Echo*, 12 November and 10 December 1991).

MY DAD GETS DOCTORED

JOE: There were a lot of Indian doctors. One I know of is Straight Hair. Straight Hair [also known as Chief Butcher] doctored my dad, where he took a curse from the ghosts out of his back. What he took out was cloth and hair. It looked like wheat. They broke it open and it was wheat. There was cloth also. That's what was making my dad very sick. A doctoring tool, they call it. They burn it at the end, and they cut you open. They took something out of my father. Soon after that he got better. He told the Old Lady to make fire and burn the thing that they took out of him. Today when somebody gets cursed by the ghosts, the doctors say, "Oh, he got a stroke."

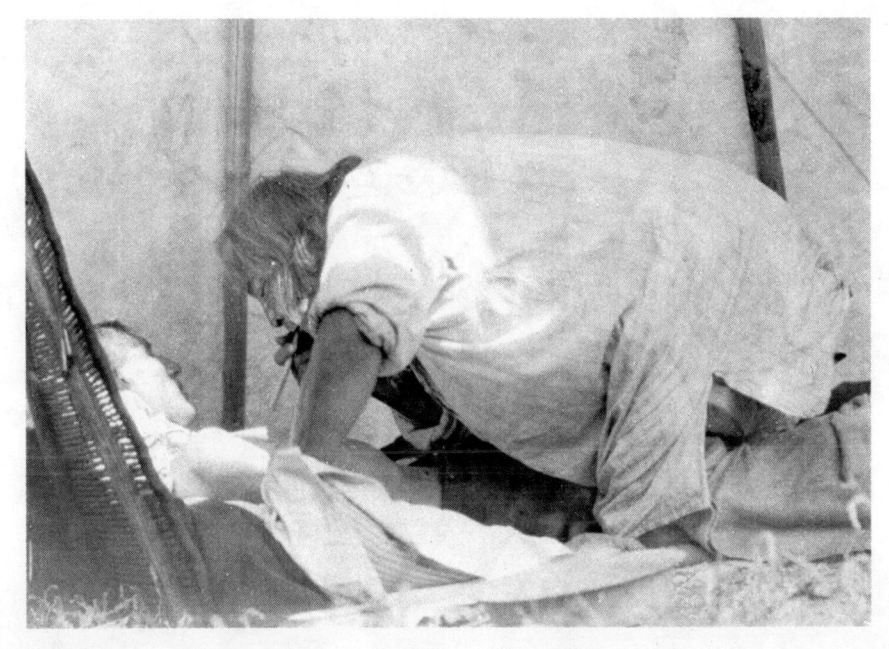

Blackfeet medicine man Awunna blowing yellow paint through a medicine whistle onto the arms and chest of Stuyimi during curing ceremony in Montana c.1905 (described in McClintock 1968: 244–50). (Yale Collection of Western Americana, Beinecke Rare Book and Manuscript Library, negative #390020337296689)

WEASEL TAIL

"Many different ways of curing were used in traditional Blackfoot society. ... [O]ne in relation to knowledge of herbs and other natural remedies practiced by skilled individuals who learned from a close relative and by their own trial and error. The other category entailed services based on more practical, mechanical knowledge, like bone setting. The last category evolved around individuals and groups who went through a formalized training process which was closely linked to their roles as ceremonialists and holders of sacred bundles" (Crowshoe and Manneschmidt, 1997: 41).

Chicken Dance Society, Blackfoot Reserve (Siksiká), 1913. L. TO R.: Heavy Shield, Pretty Young Man, Crow Shoes (the Old Man's father), One Gun, Spider Ball, Black Face, Many Shot Number 2, Philip Back Fat, Frank Sugar, last two unknown. (Harry Pollard, Provincial Archives of Alberta, P139)

Harry Pollard, born in Ontario in 1880, moved west in 1899 and established a photographic studio in Calgary. He worked for thirty years as a promotional photographer and cinematographer with Associated Screen News, travelling around the world fourteen times. His collection at the Provincial Archives of Alberta of almost twelve thousand images includes Klondike and Alberta First Nations subjects. He died in 1968 (Provincial Archives of Alberta, Harry Pollard fonds).

JOE: I tried really hard to keep our way of life going ... At the signing of Treaty 7 that's when everything started; that's where people started going their separate ways. Things started to change when the white man, the missionaries, and the priests came to start teaching our people, our children, the white man's way of life. It was in my generation when things started. When I was done school [here], I went to school for three years in Regina, Edmonton, and Calgary as a missionary. I was thinking, "Everything is so different these days."

My father did a lot of the holy ways. He was a ceremonialist. My father was transferred into the Horn Society, Medicine Pipe, the Race Horse Society, and many other societies.

"A Blackfoot person would belong to various societies in the course of his/her life. They were essential to the survival of the whole tribe and were not kin-based but reflected an individual's interest and personality. Societies [usually had] specific functions and leaders which were identified by specific [paraphernalia] and regarded as chiefs. ... Nearly all these societies were age-graded. Thus a young man started out joining the Bees, then became a member of the Mosquitoes and worked his way through the different ranks until he was a member of the Brave Dogs, the Horns or the Old Bulls. ... Based on the reduction of the population and decreased interest in traditional aspects of Blackfoot culture, many societies disappeared" (Crowshoe and Manneschmidt, 1997: 15).

My dad went to school in Calgary, [at the] religious industrial school [St. Dunstan's Calgary Industrial School]. There were others that were sent to that school: Percy Creighton, Willie Scraping White, Striped Squirrel, and there were many others that attended that school. ... At the old school across the river there was a man that used to take the boys up north to Calgary. My dad was in that group.

The "old school across the river" was the Roman Catholic Sacred Heart Residential School (est. 1898?) close to the old Peigan Indian agency buildings on the Peigan Reserve, near the north bank of the Oldman River. The boys were taken to the Church of England's St. Dunstan's Calgary Industrial School, south of Calgary, from 1896 to 1907. Scott-Brown describes what it was like to be there:

"A military form of discipline was imposed: This included wearing a uniform, having a close cropped head, military drills often with wooden weapons, and the creation of military bands with the Indian students as performers. The students were entirely immersed in Euro-Canadian culture; their own was completely ignored by the school authorities, and the use of their native language was punished. ... In these schools the boys could be taught a trade, and the 'evangilization which had begun so well on the reserves could be continued' (Report on Indian Missions, 1896). ... Being at the Calgary school was lonely for students from the southern part of Alberta, but according to Calf Robe [káínaa], it was better than being around the reserves. This was a time of hardship for native people: The buffalo had gone, farming was not that successful, there was little to do, the nomadic hunting life was being curtailed, and the people were confined to reserves" (Scott-Brown, 1987: 42, 45).

Students at St. Dunstan's Calgary Industrial School, 1897. BACK ROW L. TO R.: Mr. Young, farm instructor, ?, ?, James Starlight, Philip Back Fat, Percy Stocken (?), teacher, ?, ?, Willie Scraping White, Charles F. Pippy, carpenter. CENTRE ROW: ?, ?, John Cinespot, Charles Goodrider, Mrs. G.H. Hogbin, George H. Hogbin, principal, Nathan Many Feathers, ?, James Knowlton. FRONT ROW: far right, Percy Creighton, all others unknown. (Glenbow Archives, NA 516–1)

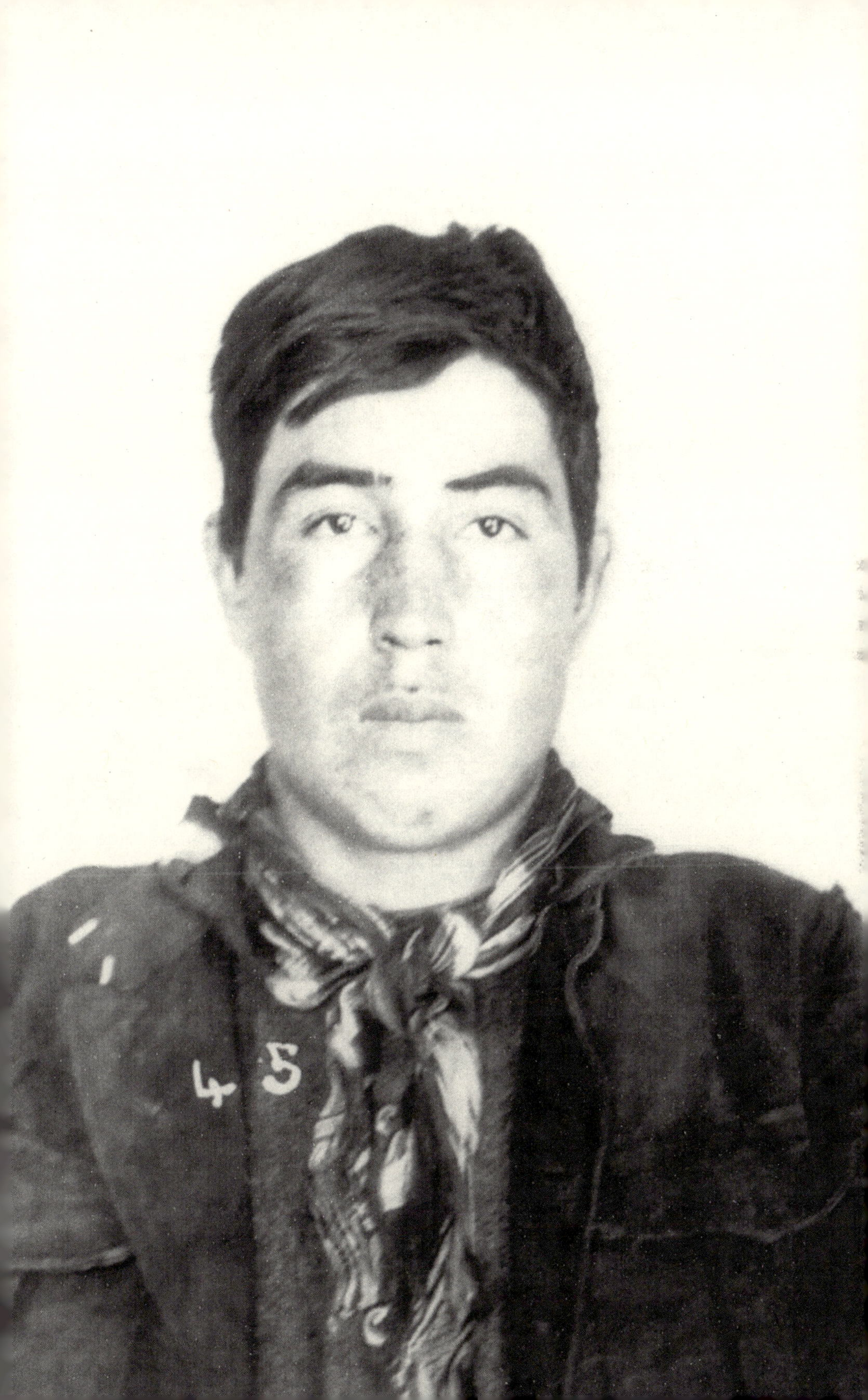
45

He learned how to build tables [the Old Man raps the table], chairs, and he was a mason. After he completed school he returned back to Brocket and worked for the agency. He worked as a maintenance person fixing stove-pipe, chairs, and tables.

RNWMP Superintendent Primrose mentions the project Willie Crow Shoes was working on in his 1908 Annual Report: "A number [of Peigans] have been steadily employed on the new agency buildings which are being put up at Brocket on the south side of the Oldman River. It is expected that these will be ready for occupation this winter" (Sessional Papers Royal Northwest Mounted Police, 1908: 65).

My father didn't have a house but he lived in tents and tipis. He moved from Wolf Flats west to Brocket. He bought a house in Brocket close to where the agency was, across from the Anglican church where Margaret Plain Eagle [the Old Man's sister] now lives. It's along Highway 3.

The old agency was located across the [Oldman] River east of where Alan Pard now lives. They moved up west when the railroad track was put in [1897–1898]. There was a lot of horse racing done at the old agency. That's where the first church was located, by the old agency. That's where the Methodists came. After they left the Anglicans came.

"Starting in 1874, seven missions were established to bring Christianity to Indians in the Fort Macleod area" (Fort Macleod History Book Committee, 1977: 12). The Reverend George McKay opened St. Peter's Church of England (Anglican) mission on the Peigan Reserve in 1878 (Glenbow Archives, Indian Missions fonds description M1356).

On previous page: Percy Shell Woman (alias Joe Martin and Percy Creighton), a Blood Indian arrested for horse stealing. Police photograph taken by the NWMP at Fort Macleod, 10 November 1904. (Glenbow Archives, NA 258–14)

On opposite page: Willie Scraping White. Photographed by W.D. Marsden, 17 January 1958. (Glenbow Archives, NA 1757–10)

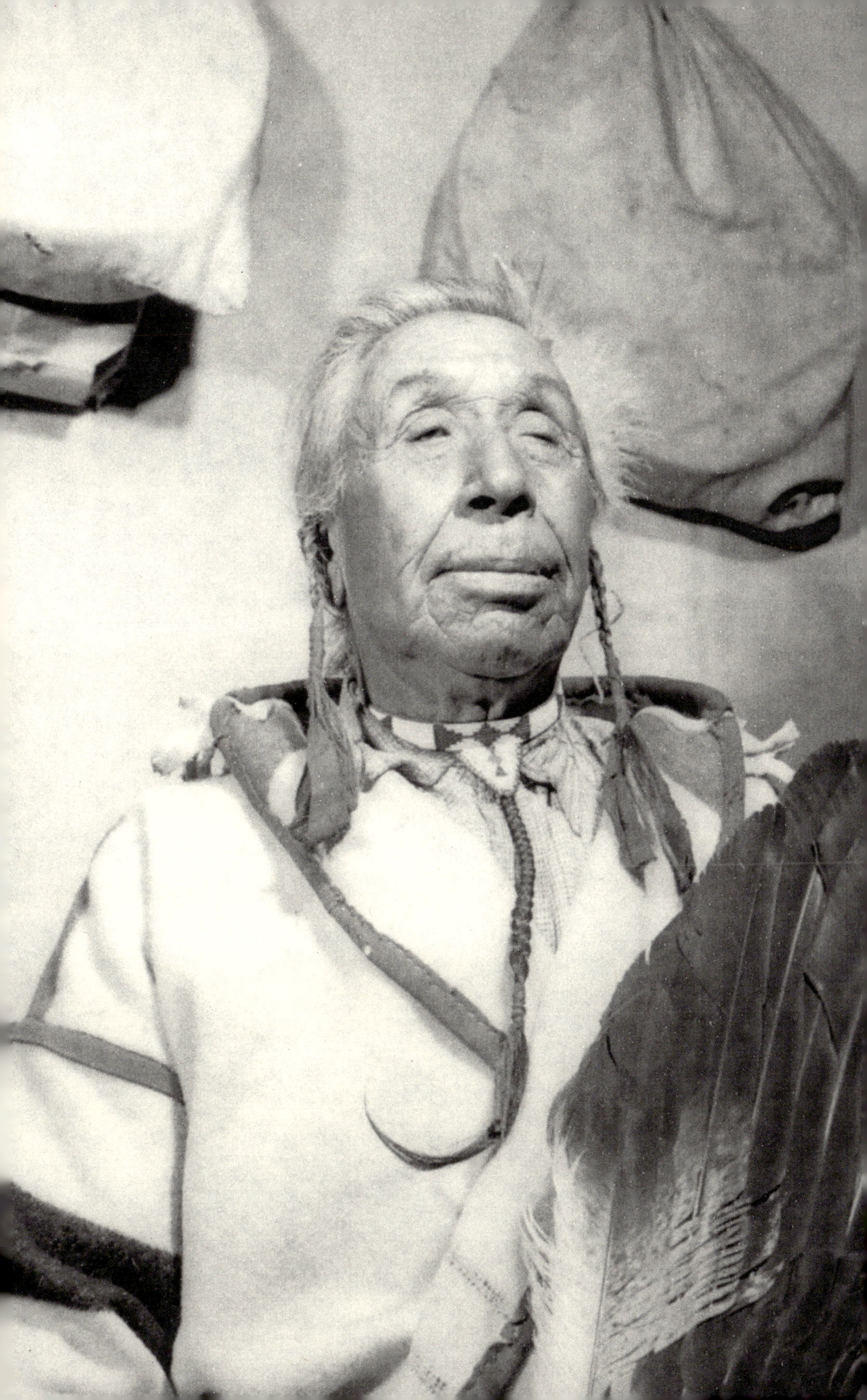

Anglican missionary the Reverend W.R. Haynes, known to Peigans as White Swan, his wife Elizabeth, Weasel Woman, and daughter Gertrude, Deer Woman, on the Peigan Reserve, c 1892. R.N. Wilson. (Glenbow Archives, NA 668-68)

Reverend (later, Canon) William Robinson Haynes (1865–1937) and his wife Elizabeth (née Edwards) (1866–1944) were Anglican missionaries. Haynes spent forty-five years among Peigans from about 1892 until he died. Their daughter Gertrude (1892–1978) grew up on the Blackfoot Reserve at Gleichen and married William Betts, farm superintendent at the Blood Reserve (Fort Macleod History Book Committee, 1977: 281–82).

The first Indian agent I knew was Mr. Graham, Rock Buffalo, and the other one was Mr. Lancaster, Rider. After [World War I], a lot of the returned men got Indian Affairs jobs. The government appointed these people to work for Indian Affairs as Indian agents. Mr. Graham and Mr. Lancaster, the Indian agents, used to attend the ceremonies. The government then told the Indian people not to practice the Indian religion anymore. The native people argued that they should continue their Indian way.

REG: **Rock Bull? [laughs]**

JOE: **Rock Buffalo.**

JOSEPHINE: **His body's like a rock.**

ONE PEOPLE

Joe: [In English] Long time ago, thousands of years ago, the old Indians are very religious, spiritual people. They like to pray, in the morning, noon, at night, the Indians thousands of years ago. But today, no more. We know, all the Indians know. Indians didn't write history. About history, no. Just today. Started today. But I think it's a good, a good thing to do, [to] write the history.

Mike: It's good that you talk on the tape because then we can write from what you say. And it's good that you sing the songs. ... Your voice will be there a hundred years from now.

Joe: Yeah, I think it's a good thing to start write history. There's so many young people misleading the other young people, [the] young generation coming up. You got to tell them the truth. You got to speak the truth from your heart.

Josephine: Today the young people, I notice they don't ... they don't tell the truth. They have to watch that. The Old Man, what he knows he tells. What he doesn't know he tells them, "I don't know the rest of that. I don't know that. That's where it stops." But where he knows he'll start. Today you have to watch that.

Mike: Are those Brave Dogs in the picture [on the wall]?

Joe: Some of them, not all of them. Some of them. I took all, all those young fellows. I talk to them. I told them, "Drinking is no good. Don't drink."

Josephine: There's one thing he said, "We never made a thing to drink, to make us go don't think, go crazy." *Náápiikoaiksi*, they ... we call that whiskey in Indian "white man's water," *náápiaohkii*, that's your water. We drink it and [makes a handsign].

MIKE: It makes people crazy.

JOSEPHINE: Yeah. They drink and drink and drink! [Claps her hands.]

JOE: You see, Mike, you take a bottle, bottle of whiskey. Up here is a butterfly. Makes you happy. Makes you feel good. Up here, butterfly. You drink. In the middle, elephant. You know elephants? Long. They never quit drinking. Down here at the bottom is the pig. You know what the pig is?

JOSEPHINE: That's what he thinks. But I wouldn't say what I think! [laughs] I don't like that stuff. Should have never be. But I don't know.

JOE: I like to work with the people. Like to talk to them. "Make a new community when you grow up. New community. Work with everybody. Work with everybody. White people, any nationality, no different. We all one people under God. We all the same."

JOSEPHINE: Just like what my grandmother told me. She said, "We believe the Creator, these ... for the *náápiikoaiksi*, for the white people, for the Indian people, for the Black people. And we shouldn't laugh at what the Black or the Indians are doing or the whites. Because it's a God-given thing. We should not laugh at, make fun of them. That's what my grandmother told me. And I believe. We have the Medicine Pipe bundle. And I was told many things that I remember. I was told that God made us. *Ápistotooki*, that's God, He made us. He gave us a religion to, to believe, to pray. And I believe that.

You know we have a Pipe, the Old Man and I have a Pipe, and every spring, when ... you hear the thunder, you unbundle. These people [George and Molly Kicking Woman] over in Browning, they come when we tell them. And nobody in the Indian way say, "I not going there. I'm not going there." That's not right. If a person can't come, [they] can't come. But a person that has a way can come, can come. Usually we have lots of people come. But we have to pay the people that unbundle. And we don't give little things … we give big things because there's only one person or two that can do that. … has to be a special person that we know that can unbundle, at the time when it's supposed to be, not any time.

MIKE: Where did the bundle come from? Who had it?

JOSEPHINE: That's his father's bundle. … These bundles come from way back.

JOE: [In English] Browning, Montana. Piikáni.

JOSEPHINE: This guy's name was Sooie. It sounds like your language, but I don't know what it is, if it's Blackfoot or *náápiikoai*. You know, I was one of the people … that laugh at these things. I was one. I laugh at. Because [when] I grew up, my mother and dad, they talk English. We go to church. I learn from church. But when I got married [in 1934], I laugh at these things. I soon found out that there was something there. … Somebody would come and tell me in a dream what it is, what I should do.

The Old Man told Sybille Manneschmidt in a 1997 interview that Sooie was Charlie Reevis (possibly Charley Revais?). The language, spelling, and meaning of Sooie is unknown (Sybille Manneschmidt to Mike Ross, personal communication, 1997).

MIKE: So that made you more of a believer?

JOSEPHINE: Then I don't make fun. I don't laugh at

things. I believe. I believe. I don't know if people years ahead will find out, but religion in the English and the Blackfoot are almost the same.

MIKE: Can you practice both? As a Peigan can you have traditional beliefs as well as Christian beliefs?

JOSEPHINE: Really, I do. They go together. I believe in the Indian religion. I believe in the *náápiikoai* religion. ... Long time ago, when two people are going to be put together, married, it takes four days. They do whatever, I don't know what they do, takes four days. But you go to a *náápiikoai* church, you get married in one day.

MIKE: When you and the Old Man were married, was it in the church or was it a combination of old ways and the Christian ways?

Tipis joined for a bundle opening at the Crowshoe's, Brocket, July 1989. (Courtesy Michael Ross)

JOSEPHINE: It was in the church, in the Anglican church. This minister, he put us together. We went through a marriage that way. I had a wedding cake and everything. But I believe. I had a faith in it. I believe the two are the same. The one we pray to God; in the Blackfoot way, *Ápistotooki*. That's the same. The one who made us, *Ápistotooki*.

THE OLD MAN LEFT THE KITCHEN AND RETURNED WITH A BOXED SET OF AUDIOCASSETTES LABELLED "SAINT JOHN'S GOSPEL AND THE ACTS OF THE APOSTLES" RECORDED IN BLACKFOOT LANGUAGE. HE SHOWED THEM TO ME.

JOE: It's the same with our native religion. It's all the same to God. This is what I want to tell the young people.

JOSEPHINE: Look, if you think of it, it means the same in the Indian way. That's the way we understood. That's why we believe in the white man's religion and the Indian religion. There's some stories that are the same, only the different ways of talking. You know what I mean? It's like they're stronger together. They're both strong.

MIKE: Did you have to go to Sunday school?

JOSEPHINE: Went to Sunday school, yeah. I got this [gestures]...

MIKE: You got slapped.

JOSEPHINE: I got to put my hands out and with a strap.

MIKE: Did the Old Man go to school?

JOE: Me? Nineteen-sixteen. Yeah.

MIKE: For how long?

JOE: **Eleven years. Nineteen-twenty-eight I came out.**

MIKE: **Was it a religious school?**

JOE: **Yeah, missionary school, Anglican, on the reserve [Victoria Jubilee Home Indian Residential School].**

MIKE: **Was it pretty good teaching? Did you enjoy school?**

JOE: **Yeah.**

MIKE: **Were you under pressure to be white and not Indian? Could you speak Blackfoot at school?**

JOE: **No. They told me, "Don't speak Blackfoot."**

Canadian laws during 1876–1986 forced thousands of Native children to attend day schools, residential schools, and industrial schools. The national system of government-owned schools operated in partnership with the Roman Catholic Church, Church of England (Anglican), Salvation Army, and Methodists and Presbyterians. Children in residential and industrial schools boarded away from their families, even if they lived close by (see Milloy 1999).

Bull Plume's winter count notes 1898 as the year "children were killed Victoria House," possibly recording the deaths of children trying to run away to their homes during the winter (Raczka, 1979: 78). Glenbow Archives holds Victoria Jubilee Home material including 1913 details of students' religious and academic instruction, diet, and required farming, livestock, gardening, kitchen, laundry, sewing, and mending chores (Glenbow Archives, Indian Mission fonds M1356).

MIKE: **Did you have to cut your hair?**

JOE: Yeah. ... I went to school [in] 1916. And my first Christmas, and I didn't know Christmas, but my first Christmas when I was a boy in residential school, and I like it.

JOSEPHINE: We had turkey, plum pudding, and all that. Candies and fruit. We [were] supposed to like it [laughs].

JOE: And [in] 1928 I want to go to Winnipeg, St. John's College in Winnipeg, but the agent, Indian Affairs, they wouldn't let me go.

MIKE: Why not?

JOE: I don't know. They said, "Grade eight is your limit." I went [to] grade eight and two years after. I wanted [to] take up the law. I wanted [to] take up the law for my people, so I can protect them. But the agent told me, "No. They don't do that."

St. John's College is a small Anglican college and, in 1877, was one of the founding colleges of the University of Manitoba.

Unidentified students at Victoria Home Indian Residential School, c.1916. The school principal, Reverend W.R. Haynes, is centre, back row. (Glenbow Archives, PA 1626-232)

MIKE: **What did you do after that?**

JOE: Farming. I started to farm. I used to farm here. It's my dad's farm, was small, but I plow it all up. I used to have pigs, milk cows, chickens, and my cattle. I had lots of cattle out on the range. I kill my beef, put it in the co-op. I got my key. I go to town, get meat.

JOSEPHINE: Yeah, when my kids were small, he kills one beef for the year. They cut it up and wrap it up and write on it, put it in a cooler. For all year I go up there I take some meat for my family.

JOE: She used to make our butter. Milk cows, take the cream, cream separate, take the cream, and she used to make butter.

Peigan farmer haying with horse team. No date. (Glenbow Archives, NA 4133–17)

Josephine: You know, I was taught all those things at school. I make butter for the family. We put it in the freezer. When we need it we put it out.

Joe: Homemade butter's good butter. I used to grow garden too. Turnips, potatoes, down here [gestures]. I dig the ground, put them in there for the winter.

Josephine: Yeah, we do that. We have a garden. We put potatoes in there, carrots, turnips, mostly. Not the other vegetables, no, mostly potatoes, carrots, turnips, onions.

Mike: Did you give the food to other people or sell it to other people?

Josephine: I don't sell. The Indian never sells, he gives.

Joe: I go and help the poor people.

Josephine: Give them, give them. Don't sell. We don't sell. But now that I've grown up, I sell it, whatever. I'm like you, *náápiikoan*!

Joe: At harvest time when I get my wheat threshed, I get grain, take it to Lethbridge. Flour mill, make flour, chop, bran.

Josephine: I remember, Mike, I'll tell you. I went with the Old Man to Macleod. They were gonna sell the pigs. Put the pigs in the back of the truck. We went down there. His pigs were the best pigs. The other pigs were skinny, and you can see they were thin. What we feed our pigs is mostly chop. Anything. Leftover food I throw out, what the pigs can eat I give to the pigs. The rest I give to the dogs. The dogs can chew at bones and stuff. But at that time his pigs were the best pigs. The *náápiikoaiksi* pigs were lower, counted lower.

MIKE: What years did you farm?

JOE: '28 up to 1940. Yeah, from '28 up to 1940 when I lease my land to Hutterites. But ... they're no good.

MIKE: Why "no good"?

JOE: They don't farm right. Last year this man put his crop in there about June. Too late. I put my crop in May, about middle of May. Needs three months to get a good crop.

MIKE: How come you stopped farming?

JOSEPHINE: Because he was, he's too old, can't farm any more. Must be in [his] sixties; he stopped.

MIKE: What were you doing in World War II?

JOE: I go out to work. I go to work in the ranches, farmers. I work. I make little money [laughs].

JOSEPHINE: Right. Working all the time that old man. He makes me get up early in the morning; I have to get up. Right. Make coffee, tea ...

JOE: You know where they feed the cattle? I worked there for two years. Feed lot [just west of Brocket]. I worked there for two years. Nineteen-forty-five I worked there. I join the Army, too, but they wouldn't take me. The agent told them, "No, we don't want Joe to go to war. He's farming here. He's a big farmer." The recruiting officers, they told me, "One farmer feeds ten soldiers in the front."

JOSEPHINE: My brothers, three of them, they went to war [Pete, Henry, and Edward]. But they came back. They died here. They didn't die at the war. They said that, "Well, he farms. We won't take him. Like, he feeds ten soldiers in the front. He farms. We'll let him do whatever. We won't take him." But they took my brothers. They weren't farmers.

Joe: They say, the Army said, "Send me a boy, I'll send you back a man." That's good. I know it. "Send me a boy, I'll send you back a man, strong man." That was good, I know.

Josephine: **That's right.**

Mike: **What was it like for you in the Depression? The 1930s.**

Joe: Pretty bad. No good. You can't get job. No money. Hard to eat. I had to hunt up in the mountains, had to hunt elk, deer. A farm, no good. One bushel of oats twenty cents a bushel. Way down. No money.

Riding the rails at Frank, in the Crowsnest Pass west of Brocket, 1930. (Glenbow Archives, NC 54-3604)

Depression. Bad years. On the track you see trains coming, bunch of people sitting up. Hobos looking for jobs.

Josephine: Yeah, we used to see a lot of that.

Mike: Would they get off here or just keep going?

Josephine: They keep going. Some get off, some that keep going. Wonder what happen, what do they do? See them lot on top of the boxcars, singing. I'll tell you one thing. I remember one time, [this] girl she was with her grandmother. She came and she made bread. And this *náápiikoan*, he's walking the highway. I went out there, and I see her. She was feeding him the bread. Came in and fold it in a paper bag and gave it to him on his way. The Old Lady came and she said, "You should not feed that guy. He's gonna come back again." But no.

Joe: You know, Mike, in Depression you have to have a coupon to buy shoes, clothes. I think it's coming again. I think it's gonna be here.

Dust storm west of Fort Macleod during the Dirty Thirties. (Glenbow Archives, NA 2928-28)

JOSEPHINE: You know, I remember the time when we had to have coupons to buy sugar. I have to have enough coupons to buy my sugar, my flour, whatever.

MIKE: When was that?

JOSEPHINE: That was during [World War II].

MIKE: Rationing.

JOE: It was hard, pretty hard. Hudson Bay Company, old Hudson Bay Company, you know it?

MIKE: Do you remember going there?

JOE: Yeah, get a blanket, get clothes, get a gun, get smoke, sugar. Indians don't know about money. [He pulls out his wallet from his back pocket and removes the paper money.] You see, Indian go in a store, Hudson Bay, and put maybe five dollars. [Lays a five-dollar bill on the table.] Sugar, maybe bread. They don't wait for change.

JOSEPHINE: Yeah, right. Long time ago. They didn't know there was change there.

JOE: Indians didn't know this until Mormons. Mormons told them, "There's change in that dollar." And then the Indians learn it. Today, you got to have a bunch of papers. [He shows me the contents of his wallet.] You go to the bank, your ID card, social [insurance] number. Bad.

MIKE: When you were a boy, did you have your own horse? Do you remember your early horses?

Fort Macleod Hudson's Bay Company store hardware department, c.1912. The store closed in 1920 and was gutted by fire in 1974. (Glenbow Archives, NA 5051–70)

The Calgary Stampede Indian Events Committee donated a three-year-old gelding for an auction to benefit 1995 Canadian All-Around Rodeo Champion Duane Daines, who had suffered a spinal cord injury while competing (*Calgary Herald*, 2 October 1995: 1).

JOSEPHINE: **He named this horse. Did you hear about it in the news?**

MIKE: **I was there!**

JOSEPHINE: **You were there? What was it, the name, in your language?**

MIKE: **I forget. When did you learn how to ride and take care of horses? How old were you?**

JOE: **About six years old [laughs].**

Fort Macleod main street looking east, decorated for the "Big Jubilee, Pageant, and Stampede" commemorating the town's fiftieth anniversary, 1–3 July 1924. (Glenbow Archives, NA 659–37)

JOSEPHINE: Spaatoas, I remember. That means high spirit. That's right, that's right. That's what he named his horse. There was one that's high-spirited. ... They had many names, those horses.

MIKE: Did your parents have a lot of horses?

JOE: Yeah, I have to break them. Some they kick, move around [laughs]. I got lots a horses from my grandma. I like horses. I like to ride. I like horses. I'm gonna buy another one maybe this year. Gonna look white. I'm gonna buy it.

MIKE: Those early horses, did they have a brand?

The Old Man naming a "Spaatoas" at a name-giving ceremony in Calgary in 1995. He later said that Spaatoas had been the name of his best working horse in the 1920s. (Photograph by Dave Olecko and published in the *Calgary Herald*, 2 October 1995: 1. Reprinted with permission of the *Calgary Herald*.)

JOE: Yeah, 70-0. About here [indicates his hip]. 'O' on the front. 'O' stands for Peigan. Yeah. 'O' for Peigan. My brand here [indicates his right shoulder]. My cattle, '218,' here [indicates his right side].

MIKE: How old were you when you started to go to rodeos?

JOE: Oh, about twenty-two.

MIKE: What events were you in?

Four

Pete LaGrandeur, Peigan ranch manager, at cattle round-up on the Peigan Reserve, 16 July 1954. The "O" on the horse's right shoulder is the Piikáni brand. (Glenbow Archives, NA 4510-551)

JOE: **Bulldog, ride bronc. I like it [laughs].**

MIKE: **Were you any good?**

JOE: **No. All of them, fall down [laughs].**

MIKE: **You're very honest!**

JOSEPHINE: **I've got three brothers that are horsemen. They love to ride. My brothers, three of them, they all have their own horses.**

Horse bunch. It's not just one horse you own in the Indian, it's a bunch a horses you own.

MIKE: Did you have a special horse for hunting?

JOE: No. Some you got a pack horse. Your blankets, your tent.

MIKE: When you went hunting, would you go for a few days?

JOE: About five days. Bring [home] the meat, give to the old people. I used to trap beavers in the Oldman River. Stay out there all night. Put my trap. In the morning, big beaver. Start skinning.

JOSEPHINE: He sells the hide of the beaver.

JOE: Make good money.

MIKE: Where would you sell the pelt?

JOE: Macleod, Edmonton. One beaver about a hundred dollars.

JOSEPHINE: That was at the time of the war. That was good selling. I'll argue with the Old Man. Sometimes they're three hundred.

MIKE: Three hundred dollars for one beaver pelt!

JOSEPHINE: If it's good, you sell it for three hundred.

> The Old Man told interviewer Dianne Meili the dream that made him stop trapping beaver: "I used to trap beaver for money, and I got bad luck one year. A mother beaver told me I didn't have any pity on her children, so she would take no pity on mine. Four days after I learned this, my boy got hurt. He almost lost his leg. So I gave my traps away. My dad did, too" (Meili, 1991: 104).

He brings home the money.

JOE: *Aapaiks*.

JOSEPHINE: [Translating] And the weasels too.

JOE: Trap weasels here. Black tail. You got to skin them good.

MIKE: Where would you trap weasels?

JOE: Right here. But no more today. No. Jackrabbits today.

MIKE: So most Peigans didn't eat rabbits?

JOSEPHINE: No.

MIKE: Why not?

JOSEPHINE: I don't know. The Indian people are very particular in what they eat. They don't eat any kind of an animal. Only the animals that you eat is deer, elk, that's all. Rabbits, no.

MIKE: Do they eat birds traditionally?

JOSEPHINE: No.

MIKE: They didn't eat fish?

JOE: They eat a lot of fish. I like fish. I catch pike. Bit of wire, get a stick, put the wire, throw them off. Great big pike [laughs].

JOSEPHINE: He shouldn't tell you that!

MIKE: Did you go ice fishing?

JOE: Yeah, ... I had to cut the ice.

MIKE: Did you go fishing in the summer?

JOE: Yeah. Go [pick] big berries too. ... saskatoons, chokecherry. ... Good [laughs].

JOSEPHINE: I ate berries and saskatoons, chokecherries. I eat that. We still do that now. If you come to our pipe dance you have some [saskatoon] berry soup.

MIKE: All this talk about food is making me hungry. Should we stop now? Should we stop for a while?

TALKING ABOUT GHOSTS
JOSEPHINE: We believe in ghosts, we do.

MIKE: I've never been bothered by a ghost.

JOSEPHINE: Do you want to find out?

MIKE: No!

JOSEPHINE: You go to a graveyard, especially the old Indian graveyard, you take a bone from there, maybe a hand. It'll bother you.

MIKE: I've heard people say that in the [Oldman River] valley they hear voices sometimes.

JOSEPHINE: I heard one. One time I was walking to Brocket from the farm place. We were walking down this road that they call Fishburn. We were walking down, my mother and I and the little kids. And I heard crying. I heard crying. And I heard it from a certain place. Somebody's gone. Somebody's crying. But nobody. Few days after that time I heard it, there was a death.

MIKE: **Has the Old Man heard ghosts?**

JOSEPHINE: **Yeah, he's experienced many like that.**

MIKE: **Is it a good thing or a bad thing for him?**

JOSEPHINE: **It's not so good because when I heard that thing, few days after there was really death. So I don't say it's a good thing. I say, myself, it's not good. It's a bad thing. I heard this crying at Man Who Smokes [?]. A few days after that, there really was death. When they put me through Sun Dance and this Old Lady, the one that always holds the Sun Dance, she put me through, she says, "You are not supposed to tell anything that's not true. You have to tell the truth. And you're not supposed to look at men in a certain way." There's many things they told me I'm not supposed to be if I'm going to go through and hold a Sun Dance. People will say, "This is the Sun Dance woman." I gotta be good. I got to do things right.**

"Both men and women had important ritual roles in ceremonies and women were central players in the Okan (Sun Dance) and partners in some of the more important societies. ... [O]nly a virtuous woman who had been faithful to her husband held prestigious positions and responsibilities in regards to society offices or sacred bundles" (Crowshoe and Manneschmidt, 1997: 18). And, from her own footnote: "Women from wealthy families who were also in the position to take care of sacred objects according to cultural expectations were sometimes re-married or divorced" (Ibid.: 80).

MIKE: You put up a Sun Dance a long time ago didn't you?

JOSEPHINE: I think it was in the thirties or in forties.

MIKE: When did you start again?

JOSEPHINE: I never quit. I'm always that woman. You never stop.

MIKE: Were there years when there was no Sun Dance?

JOE: There was many, many years there's no Sun Dance.

MIKE: What did the church think of the Sun Dance?

JOSEPHINE: The church [she gestures].

MIKE: Did they try and stop it? They just said it was crazy?

JOSEPHINE: They didn't say it was crazy. "You're not supposed to do that," is what I was told. But I know what I was doing. His [the Old Man's] grandmother gave us the Sun Dance bundle, and I still got it. [Josephine speaks in Blackfoot to the Old Man.] Go with him and he'll show you the bundle. [The Old Man takes me to their bedroom and shows me the Sun Dance bundle hanging on the wall.]

Many missionaries, mounted police, and government officials considered Sun Dances as heathen practices standing in the way of "civilizing" First Nations' people, and the Indian Act officially prohibited them as "give-away" ceremonies. The passing of a generation of knowledgeable, experienced elders and traditional rights-holders threatened survival of the Sun Dance. Josephine Crowshoe obtained transferred rights to the *Naatoas* bundle from Mrs. Rides-at-the-Door (Blood) in 1977 and, together with her husband, revived the Sun Dance.

Four

CROW SHOE GETS HIS NAME

JOE: He went south into the States to the Crow Agency and had a battle with the Crows. Crow Shoe's moccasins were worn out pretty badly and he laid alongside the Crows as the battle was going on. As the Crows left, he picked some of the moccasins up and stood up and held them to the sun and said, "My name is going to be 'Crow Shoe'." So when he came back home he told the people how he got his name "Crow Shoe" by taking the Crow's moccasins.

JOSEPHINE: [To Reg] Now you know how you got your name.

JOE: [In English] That's what they call, "coup, coup."

Crow Agency is tribal headquarters of the Crow tribe on the Crow Indian Reservation in south-central Montana near Billings.

The Old Man's paternal great-grandfather, the first Crow Shoe, pictured here in a group of Peigans and North West Mounted Police at an 1886 Peigan Sun Dance. Standing L. TO R.: Sgt. Gaigen, Runs Among Buffalo, Kidney, Crow Shoe, Running Wolf (aka, Brings Down the Sun), Jerry Potts, others unknown. FRONT L. TO R.: Good Young Man, Little Plume, Running Eagle, Shining Double, Bull Plume, Green Grass Bull, and Black Chief. (Glenbow Archives, NA 2928-53)

Five

ℬROCKET

15 February 1996

MIKE ROSS RECORDED THE FOLLOWING INTERVIEW IN BROCKET ON 15 FEBRUARY 1996. THE OLD LADY AND THE OLD MAN SPOKE ENGLISH.

Joe: **Hey Mike, long time ago the Peigans here have a powwow all the time. Social gathering. They get to know each other. They work together. Young fellas and the old people. In wintertime, snow on the ground. They danced. Is long time ago. ... From up north, Saskatchewan, Manitoba, they all come. BC, come.**

Mike: **How did they come?**

Joe: **On the train. Passenger train comes here.**

Josephine: **I've heard that. People come in from the North. They get off, the passengers, to go to powows.**

Josephine Crowshoe (née Warrior) was baptized in 1917. Her birth records are with Oblate papers available through the Provincial Archives of Alberta. Her family's names and ages are noted on Peigan Indian Agency treaty payment lists (see, for example, the 1923 list in Glenbow Archives, M1826 f.11). The Old Lady died on 31 January 2002.

JOE: I think, Mike, I think Blackfoot is going to go. There'll be no more Blackfoot. The young generation are learning different today.

JOSEPHINE: They starting to learn in school, Blackfoot. There's Blackfoot teachers now.

JOE: Say Mike, if the white people understand my Native people, they will understand the way of the Indians in the future. In the future, we're all going to work together. The only difference is language. English and Blackfoot is different. So I don't like to see my Blackfoot go. I want to hold [on to] my tongue.

Peigan tea dance, 6 June 1905. Among the onlookers, several, looking back at the camera, are costumed members of an American all-Black vaudeville troupe. (Glenbow Archives, NA 5310-1)

The touring troupe's 3 June 1905 performance at Calgary's Lyric Theatre was advertised as "a jingling musical comedy, 35 coloured artists. The largest company ever seen in Western Canada. 5 big vaudeville acts. New and catchy music. Large chorus of pretty Octoroons, very handsomely costumed. Complete scenic and lighting effects. Special augmented orchestra" (*Calgary Herald*). They played the Lethbridge Opera House, near Fort Macleod, the night before this photograph was taken (*Lethbridge News*, June 1905). Tea Dances were drinking contests popular among some tribes on the Canadian Plains in the early 1900s (Hungry Wolf, 1983).

JOSEPHINE: **That's right.**

JOE: You take French down in Quebec. They speak French all over. Write in French. Holding their culture. But we are now cross-culture, now cross-culture. I'm teaching you my culture. You teach me your culture. So we can be the same.

MIKE: Do you think white people would understand Blackfoot people better if they spoke their language?

JOE: Some white people speak Blackfoot. They good. They understand the Indians good.

JOSEPHINE: This thing I must say. We understand *náápiikoais*, your way. We understand, but you don't understand me.

MIKE: And you think language is key to understanding?

JOSEPHINE: Yeah, but I don't know.

JOE: You see, the Old People, the Old People one time told me, "If you think like a white man, you're gonna die like a white man. If you think like an Indian, you're gonna die like an Indian." That's why I get my white people come, governments come, when I open up my bundle over here. I want them to see it. I want them to learn it. We all pray to one God above. We're no strangers, you and me. All the same to God.

JOSEPHINE: I must say right now what my grandmother taught me, and my mother. We believe that God made all people and He gave us a religion, a way to talk, "You talk like …" The white people, He gave them a religion, "You pray like this, talk like that." The Indians, "You pray like this, you talk like this." The Black people, He gave them a way.

The Chinese people, He gave them a way. I believe it. My grandmother told me. And I believe it. And I pray too. I was taught the white man's religion when I was small. I grew up with it. I prayed that way. And I pray my own way. Because I learned it, I grew up with it. Right now I'll tell you if you're doing something that is not in my religion. I'll tell you, if you were going to do it in my house, I'll say, "No. That's not right. You're not supposed to do that in the house because it is an Indian house and this is the belief."

JOE: *Áa*, Mike. Our old people raised their children very disciplined. You go someplace and tell the children, "Don't touch nothing in that, don't …" I know I used to go Hudson Bay store. Me, I used to stand there and watch my dad, my mother, buy. That's why old Indians said, "If you think like a white man, you die like a white man." Alcohol, drinking, smoking dope. Not living right. …

When I have my sweat here, when I'm having sweat, I talk to the boys about the sweat, about God, about praying, about being good. All the time. I like my sweat. School teachers they come and sweat … oh, hot [laughs].

The regular Peigan sweat lodge is a low, domed structure built with interlaced willow branches made light-tight with a covering of tarps and blankets. "[S]weats can be used by anybody like a sauna or just for cleansing. But a healing sweat can only be conducted by someone who has received transfer rites in the physical form of a tipi design, an individual sacred bundle which might be part of a society, or a ceremonial bundle" (Crowshoe and Manneschmidt, 1997: 33).

MIKE: **Did you do sweats when you were a younger man?**

JOE: When I was a young man [on my birthday], they throw me in the water. Cold! I had to learn to swim myself. Water's cold. Young babies, they have a bath, cold water. Make you strong. You don't get sick. No. You go

Willow ribs of the Old Man's sweat lodge, Brocket, 1989. (Courtesy Michael Ross.)

in the water. Cold. *Áa*, it's good. Up here, warm. In the wintertime you go outside, snow. You take the snow, wash your face. I done that, me.

JOSEPHINE: But now he's at the age he's a *náápiikoan* now. He doesn't do that anymore. He can't do it. He'll get sick.

JOE: I sweat up north, way up north, Saddle Lake. I sweat twenty-five below. Is cold. Twenty-five below. Big snow. Cold. Few years ago. You come out, you feel fresh. I broke my leg. I broke them. The Old Man fix them up. I had a cast. My father cut it open, and he fix my leg. Was good. I can walk. The doctor told me, "Joe, you should never take your cast off. You're gonna [be] lame." Says, "One year from now, gonna see you." So he saw me playing football, soccer. He says, "How's your leg?" I told him, "It's alright."

JOSEPHINE: He took the cast off. He said to me he took the cast off, put his leg over the sweat, over the rock, hot, hot rock in the water. No more sore. And covers the leg up in a blanket.

JOE: Opened my cast. It was hot. He gonna cut it. My dad, he bought vinegar. He put vinegar and he cut it open. And my leg started to shake.

MIKE: Because [it was] cold?

JOE: No. It's my nerves, my nerves. When he took it off, the doctor said, "I gonna put a cast [on]." I said, "No. No more cast. So heavy. No more cast." I was alright. I ride around. I walk all over.

MIKE: How did you break your leg?

JOE: A horse, riding a horse. He slipped.

MIKE: How old were you when that happened?

JOE: In about '23 [twelve years old].

MIKE: Do you remember your friends that you hung around with when you were that age?

JOE: Yeah, we used to do lot of riding all over, down the bush. Go fishing on a horse. We go in the water, fish. I like. Used to go hunting deer, elk, and moose up in the mountains. Seen a bear up there, great big bear.

JOSEPHINE: I remember the time he went to water the horses. He came back with a stick he put the fish [on]. He snared the fish, great big fish. He brought them. I cleaned them and put them away.

MIKE: What were the Indian agents like here on the reserve?

JOE: Some are good, some are tough, very tough. Returned soldiers after the war, 1914. All the returned soldiers could come and [get] jobs. Teachers, principals at the school, agency, all returned men. When we don't like our agent, we sign petitions. [Slaps his hand on the table.] We kick him out.

MIKE: Did that happen?

JOE: Yeah, we sign petitions. Send it to the government. The government said back, "It's okay. Your chief and counsellors and the Peigan, you want to get rid of him, just say yes." So they said they told him he's too tough.

MIKE: What kinds of things would make them tough?

JOE: At the office, at the office all the records, books, all the records are wrong. I know. I had some money there. I went to the agent. I told him, "I want to find out my money. How much money I got in here?" He said, "You got none." So I got another paper in my pocket. I open it. I show him. He said, "Okay. You come back tomorrow, come back tomorrow." Next day I went there. He said, "No. Tomorrow, tomorrow, tomorrow." All no good.

MIKE: Do you remember the agent's name?

JOE: [Says a name in Blackfoot translated as Running Eagle] Mr. Arthur.

JOSEPHINE: He died a long time ago.

MIKE: Were there good agents as well?

Chester A. Arthur and wife Elisabeth Crocker Arthur, c. 1914. Peigans called him Running Eagle. (Glenbow Archives, PA 3280-1)

JOE: No. ... Some are good.

MIKE: What would make them good?

JOE: They make you crop. They make you work. They give you job, work. They get lots to eat. You get hungry, you go to the agent. He write a note. Take it to the store and buy groceries. Was good. She knows.

JOSEPHINE: You know, when we first married I got some dishes, I got a tent, I got a stove. I got many things. But [the Old Man] had to pay for them through his farm work. He pays for these things.

JOE: Today, no work for the young people today. Should be, should be lot of work today, lot.

JOSEPHINE: We still have an agent. We used to have a person that writes. We call him in our Indian language The Man that Writes.

MIKE: Where was the agency located? Was it down in the river valley?

JOE: No. Up here.

JOSEPHINE: If it was down there it would have been washed away! I remember when there was water from this bank to the other bank. Water all the way. You could see the houses'—what do you call it?—pipes showing. All covered. We don't stay there during the flooding times in the spring. I used to live down there when I was small. My dad used to live there. I remember when the water came. Everybody went on top.

MIKE: Do you remember a really bad flood in 1923?

JOSEPHINE: There was water from one bank to the other, all water, was all the way through. And the houses were covered. No houses. That was when I was small. And when the water went down, we went down to see our

Chester A. Arthur (1876–1929) was agricultural inspector for the Peigan Reserve and Peigan Indian agent from 1923 to 1929 (Glenbow Archives, Arthur family fonds, M8188).

house. And in the front door, the doorstep, threw it open, there was a great big frog under there. [Claps her hands.] I remember those times.

MIKE: [To the Old Man] Do you remember some of the guys you would hang around with when you were a young man? People like "Judge" McLaughlin? Did you know him when you were really young?

JOE: Really young, about seven, eight years old. I knew "Judge." We used to go out riding horse, round up cattle. Yeah, I know him. He's my friend, my big friend "Judge." You know, Mike, "Judge" McLaughlin used to come down here when I open up my Pipe. He used to come here. He and I, we'll sit there and talk, talk, talk about the old ways out there.

Frank Richard "Judge" McLaughlin (1911–1993), was a second-generation Pincher Creek area rancher. From his obituary: "Judge was synonymous with horses and ranching. In addition to operating the ranch at Beaver Mines, he worked for 25 years as a stock rider for the Castle River Stock Association. His love for horses and rodeos was exceeded only by his love for people as evidenced by his numerous friends. He was especially fond of his many native friends from the Peigan Reserve whom he admired and respected" (*Lethbridge Herald*, 27 December 1993: D2).

JOSEPHINE: I remember that. "Judge" used to come and they would talk about old times.

MIKE: Do you remember other boys you used to hang around with? Are they still around?

JOE: They're all gone. Arnold Prairie Chicken, Edward Meat Face. Oh, there's a whole lot. They're gone. We used to ride around, whole bunch, on Sunday. Sundays used to come, we used to go riding.

JOSEPHINE: The rest, the weekdays, are working days. Sunday is a day they ride around and do things.

MIKE: Did you ever get into trouble?

JOSEPHINE: Lots of trouble. [Translating for the Old Man] Says, "No. Boys never were caught by police and stuff." You know, one time, he was telling us, at that school, at the old school, they had something like that …

MIKE: A heat register.

Peigans at Brocket in 1923, including the Old Man's older brother Jack and several friends, his mother's second husband, Joe Buffalo, and the Old Lady's half-brother, Bernard Bastien. FRONT ROW, L. TO R.: Sacred Owl, Edward Meat Face, Jack Crowshoe, Tom Yellow Horn Jr., Willie David. MIDDLE ROW, L. TO R.: John English, Little Leaf, Philip Big Swan, Chief Tom Yellow Horn, Joe Medicine Calf. BACK ROW, L. TO R.: Joe Buffalo, Bernard Bastien, Jim Small Legs, Charlie Strikes With A Gun, Victor North Peigan, Morning Bull, Red Young Man, and Jim Morning Bull. (Glenbow Archives, NA 5508-1)

JOSEPHINE: Yeah. He said we took the thing, we took it off. He said this man, he was a principal, he comes in with his whip, [saying] "Anybody who moves or talks …" So they did that. He said we took that thing off, we put a rug there. He comes in with his whip … and he came and he just fell [laughs]. He said he was standing there. How can we help him, he's way down there! I said look what he did long time ago. Today, we say his grandchildren do bad things but they never did thing like that! Yeah. Those were the bad things he did!

MIKE: When you went to school, was it a day school or a boarding school?

JOE: Boarding school. I stayed there.

MIKE: You couldn't live at home when it was so close by? When did you come home?

JOE: Never come. We go camping at Coleman, way up in the mountains [in the Crowsnest Pass west of Brocket]. We don't come home. All the kids go up there.

MIKE: Could your parents visit you when you were at school?

JOE: Yeah, on the weekends. Saturday they come. I glad to see them. They go to church in there with me.

MIKE: At the school?

JOE: Yeah, they go to church on Sunday.

MIKE: How would they come down there?

JOE: Wagon team. Horses.

MIKE: What was the name of the school?

JOE: Victoria Home. It was the second school on the reserve. The first school was down the [Oldman] river, way down there. And then they move up here [Pincher Creek]. And then they move up here too [Brocket].

MIKE: They moved out of the valley and up onto the prairie?

JOE: [Yes]. Quite a change for the kids. Down the river it's good. You could go fishing, swimming, skating wintertime, hike. But not out here.

MIKE: Did they give you holidays?

Boys at Victoria Jubilee Home Indian Residential School, c. 1910s. (Glenbow Archives, PA 1626–230)

Deaconess Stapleton and Victoria Jubilee Home schoolchildren in 1920. (General Synod Archives, Anglican Church of Canada MSCC-Residential School Collection, P7538-398)

JOE: Yeah.

MIKE: Could you go to your family?

JOE: Yeah.

MIKE: Like Christmas?

JOE: No, in June. Just four weeks.

MIKE: Would you get breaks?

JOE: Yeah.

MIKE: For a couple of weeks?

JOE: Yeah.

MIKE: Was it a pretty good school?

JOE: Yeah, Christmas tree. You know that railroad bridge? Up back in there we cut Christmas tree. We all go up there with a sleigh. We put, we bring it home. Cut two trees. Was good.

MIKE: Who were the trees for?

JOSEPHINE: They were for the school. There was one tree where the children all go; it must be in the dining room. They decorate that tree and one in the class. I remember one time when the little ones all had dolls. I didn't get no doll. The, whatever, couldn't afford dolls. So I got mad at Santa Claus. Today I'm still mad at Santa Claus [laughs]! I remember one Christmas the girls got dolls. I got a boy doll and a girl doll. The boy doll had all knitted clothes on. That was good. And the girl doll had dresses, nice fancy dresses. That was good. I got to play with my dolls. I had two dolls. I remember that. Long time ago, I still remember. I must have been about ten years old. We don't get dolls after fifteen. No dolls. We're not interested in dolls anymore.

MIKE: What kind of presents would you get for Christmas?

JOE: We get mitts, cap, skates, hockey stick.

MIKE: Did you learn a lot at the school that was useful?

JOE: Yeah, was a good school down there. Good. In the morning you go exercise. You run. In the morning, you go out, exercise. Jump. Skate. You take exercise is good. Outside. You got dumb-bell. Young boys, older boys, big boys all separate.

MIKE: What were the school camping trips like?

JOE: School camp was pretty hard. You gotta go fishing [to] eat. You gotta go fish. Bring some fish and the cook cook them for you.

MIKE: Did all of the boys go or just the older boys?

JOE: All the boys. Everybody go. Four weeks. July. August you come back to school.

MIKE: When did you get to stay with your parents if you were at the school then at school camp?

JOSEPHINE: I must say something. I remember weekdays the parents come and visit their children. We never leave that school until the summer holidays. Then we go home for four weeks. Only the little girls. The big girls stay at the school. That's what happens. We go home. After the month is over then we go back to the school. The big girls stay at home. Like he said, they [the boys] went camping.

MIKE: Were you happy to go back to school after the break?

JOE: Yeah, I was happy to go back to school.

MIKE: How come?

JOE: I don't like camping.

MIKE: Do you remember getting treaty money there in Fort Macleod?

JOE: In Brocket, just five dollars.

MIKE: Did you go up to the Calgary Stampede when you were a young man?

JOE: Yeah.

JOSEPHINE: One year we used to have camp there. We used to have our tipi and everything. And it rained and water came in and spoiled all the rugs that I had. They're bear rugs and cow rugs. Really spoiled my things and mattresses and blankets, spoiled everything. I seen in the paper, it says, "The Crowshoe was mad."

JOE: Hey, Mike. Calgary Stampede. The old people would talk up there. They have a place, a big building. [We] went there. We all go in there, have coffee, doughnuts. We all talk. Tape recorder's good in there. Calgary. Sarcee, Stoney, Blackfoot, Bloods, and the Peigans, five tribes in there. Old people talk up there.

Brocket Trading Company c.1924. (Glenbow Archives. PA 3280-4)

MIKE: **How old were you when you went to your first Stampede?**

JOE: **[In] about '28.**

MIKE: **Did your parents go before?**

JOE: **They went there before. They went in 1911; 1911 to 1920. They quit.**

JOSEPHINE: **They're too old I guess.**

The first Calgary Stampede was held in 1912. It toured Winnipeg and New York, returning to Calgary in 1919 as a special Victory Stampede marking the end of World War I. The Calgary Stampede became an annual event in 1923. Keith Regular writes about the history of Native participation in such events: "During the late 19th and early 20th centuries, when agricultural exhibitions and fairs became commonplace in southern Alberta, the participation of local Indian tribes was usually solicited. These events, sometimes spanning several days, were originally intended to be promotional affairs, designed to exhibit the latest in agricultural technology, local crafts and work, and to publicize the benefits of living in that particular area. ... Invariably, the invitation to Indians was enthusiastically received. The Natives were only too glad to escape the confines of their respective reserves and the domination of the Indian agents. ... Probably more important for the Indians were the provisions they received in payment for their participation. These usually came in the form of sugar, flour, tea and meat, and were a welcome supplement to the often meager rations received from their reserves" (Regular, 1986: 1, 2).

Six

BROCKET

3 April 1996

MIKE ROSS RECORDED THE FOLLOWING IN BLACKFOOT ON 3 APRIL 1996. JOSEPHINE AND REG CROWSHOE WERE ALSO PRESENT. JIMMY STRIKES WITH A GUN TRANSLATED IN DECEMBER 1999.

CHOOSING MY INDIAN WAY

JOE: Today I know the spiritual way very well. When I left school in 1928, I was going to become a white man at that time, to be a missionary, a priest. So they brought me down to Prince Albert [Saskatchewan]. That's where I stayed. They brought me down to Manitoba, and I got to know how the Crees lived. A lot of those people, the Crees, were very poor the way they lived. Then I came back home. When I came home they told me, "You have to go to Banff [Alberta] where you will be sworn in as a priest." I started to Banff. When I got to Banff I started to worry. The priests had a meeting and they called upon me. They told me to sit in the middle. They told me, "You're sitting on the 'hot seat' now. We're going to ask you the Indian way and the white man's way." And I told them that wasn't the reason why I came there. The reason why I came was that I was going to be sworn

This was a very significant story for the Old Man. A version was given as his eulogy at his memorial service in Brocket on 28 October 1999.

in as a priest. One of the priests got up and came over to me and said, "Joe, go back home, gather all your bundles, your ceremonial stuff, and burn them. When they're all burnt you can come back and you can become a priest." I had really mixed feelings. I just sat there and I was thinking. I thought about it all night long. That morning, I didn't have breakfast. I told them I'd go in there the next day at three. So I sat and I prayed. Then I knew what I could tell them.

So, at three o'clock I went back to the church and I stood outside and I looked at this beautiful church. I went inside the church and sat down where they sat me before. The priests came in and they started praying. They asked me, "What are you going to say?"

"Yesterday you told me to go home and burn all my ceremonial stuff and to quit praying, to give up my way of life. The Creator, Jesus, didn't say that. All religions are sacred, are holy. All you priests stay in school for six, seven years to become a priest. Yesterday you guys told me to burn all my holy ceremonial stuff. You said this, not me. I'm going to tell you priests today, each of you priests take some kerosene and pour it around the church and burn it. After it burns to the ground, then I will go home and take my ceremonial stuff and burn them also. When you told me to burn my ceremonial stuff I was thinking and praying. I don't know why I thought about it. If I burn my ceremonial stuff it will be just like burning all of my elders [of] the past and today."

And then I remembered I should have told the priests about the church, how nice the church was, and to tell me about all the statues that were in there, to tell me stories about them. After I told them what I had to say, the priests didn't say anything; they just sat there. I told them, "I'm going to go outside. You guys can say whatever you want." I went outside and they followed and asked me to come back in. I went back in and they told me, "What you told us is really hard, what you said, you'll be just like burning your people. The same for the church. People that come to church, we'll be burning those people also. People will be lonely if the church burns." They told me, "You'll still be working for the church." Cuthand was there. Stan Cuthand told me, "I'll go back and forth from Stand Off to Brocket to help you in your work."

Stan Cuthand, Plains Cree, was born on the Little Pine Reserve near North Battleford, Saskatchewan, in 1914. He was ordained an Anglican priest in 1945 and served as a missionary in various communities, including the Blood Reserve in Alberta. He has worked as a translator and professor of culture and history: "A lot of healing comes from knowing who you are, knowing your identity. And the Cree language, the culture, is how you get the concepts. Then you understand yourself, and you understand the old people and why they say certain things. It's all based on the language. You can't separate language and culture" (www.anglicanjournal.com/127/08/canada06.html). See also "Sailing Horses," a CBC "Ideas" radio program about Cuthand broadcast in May 2002.

One day I was plowing my field when Stan Cuthand came and said, "The priests in Banff want you to go back up there so that you can be inducted into the priesthood." I said, "Well, I think I should tell the truth. I think I should stay home. I think it's better for me to do my Indian way." About eight years later, I met Stanley Cuthand in Lethbridge and we were talking. Stan Cuthand mentioned to me that he had also quit the priesthood and gone back to his way of life.

I kept dreaming about our way of life. I went to Siksiká. There was a person there named Small Eyes. Paul Weasel Walker, Herbert Lawrence [Small Eyes], and Big Kidney were there. They were priests and I met them at the hospital. I sat down, and the priest, he was an Indian who couldn't speak English and couldn't read or write, he told me, "I'm going to tell you about a dream I had two nights ago. I saw two

Morris Brass had two pipes — a Beaver Bundle Pipe and a Thunder Medicine Pipe Bundle Pipe. It is not known to which pipe the Old Man is referring (Reg Crowshoe personal communication to Sybille Manneschmidt, January 2006).

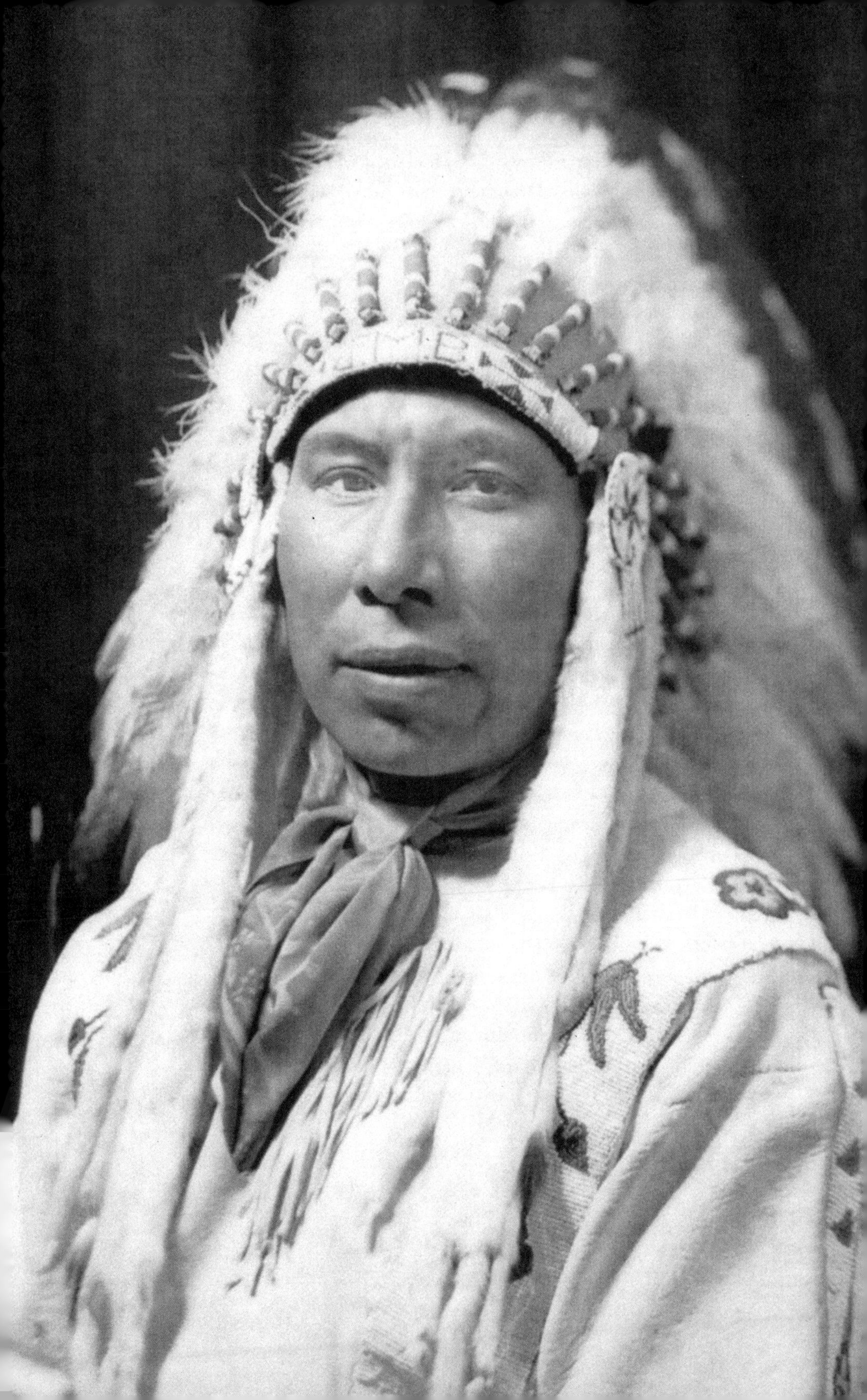

trees: one was white and the other one was green. The green tree had water around it. This person said, 'This is your way of life and the other one isn't.' So I'm going to go back now to my Pipe." It's the one Morris Brass had.

FACE PAINT

JOE: Well, this face paint. The person who has gone through Sun Dance ceremonies, All-night Smoke ceremonies and has transferred rights, he was the one that can paint faces. Right now red paint is really strong. It came from the earth. That's why, when you sing the holy song, the words in it say, "The ground is holy." [It's like] the Bible story, when Moses was told by Creator to go to the homes, "Wherever there's a home with a cross with blood you don't bother it." That's how strong it is. The same strength, this red paint.

Ceremonialists make a kind of red paint by mixing mineral ochre and animal fat on their palm. They paint with their fingers on a person's forehead, nose, cheeks, and wrists, the exact pattern depending on the ceremony and the painted person's role and status. Holy face paint is not ornamental but, rather, enables Creator to recognize a person and can symbolize the transfer of certain ceremonial rights. Crowshoe and Manneschmidt discuss the significance of face paint and show two examples in *Akak'stiman* (1997: 30–31).

JOSEPHINE: **That's right.**

JOE: **And right now I have had a lot of different dreams and spiritual messages. This Old Man dreamt and the Spirit People told him, "There's seven cows walking by. They were so skinny. They were starving. They didn't have anything to eat." And it wasn't too long, in**

On opposite page: Studio portrait of the Old Man by Gordon Crighton, 15 January 1951. (Glenbow Archives, NB 44-4b)

another direction, there were [another] seven cows. When he looked at them in his dream, they were all fed and fat. And the Old Man in his dream told him, "You know what that means?"

He said, "No."

The Old Man said, "In seven years we're gonna be poor. The cows are gonna be starving. We're gonna have nothing to eat. And when that period ends the next seven cows are gonna be well fed and chubby. Those are going to be the next seven years. We're gonna have lots to eat."

Right now you can recognize it today. Sometimes the crops are good for a long time, then sometimes the crops are not so good. It's really hard for our young people to understand our Indian way of life. When I was a young man I heard it as a story.

A similar story in the King James Bible, Genesis 41, tells the Pharaoh's dream of being by the river and beholding seven fat-fleshed, well-favoured kine (cows) followed by seven ill-favoured and lean-fleshed kine, and, in a second dream, of seeing seven full and good heads of grain and seven others withered, thin, and scorched by the wind. The Biblical prophet Joseph interprets these two dreams as representing seven years of great plenty followed by seven years of famine.

KSISOHKSISIIKSI: MOSQUITOES

JOE: There was this man named Bad Eagle. His boy got sick. The man told his boy to sit there and the boy replied that there were a lot of mosquitoes. The Old Man told him, "Just sit there." So he sat there and the Old Man started praying. As he was sitting there, the mosquitoes started landing on his face. He kept pushing them away. And the Old Man told him, "Don't push them away." Then the Old Man used face paint on the boy so that the mosquitoes wouldn't come any more. The mosquitoes sucked out all the blood and the boy was okay.

On opposite page: Crighton's photograph of the Old Man, 3 March 1958. (Glenbow Archives, 44–711)

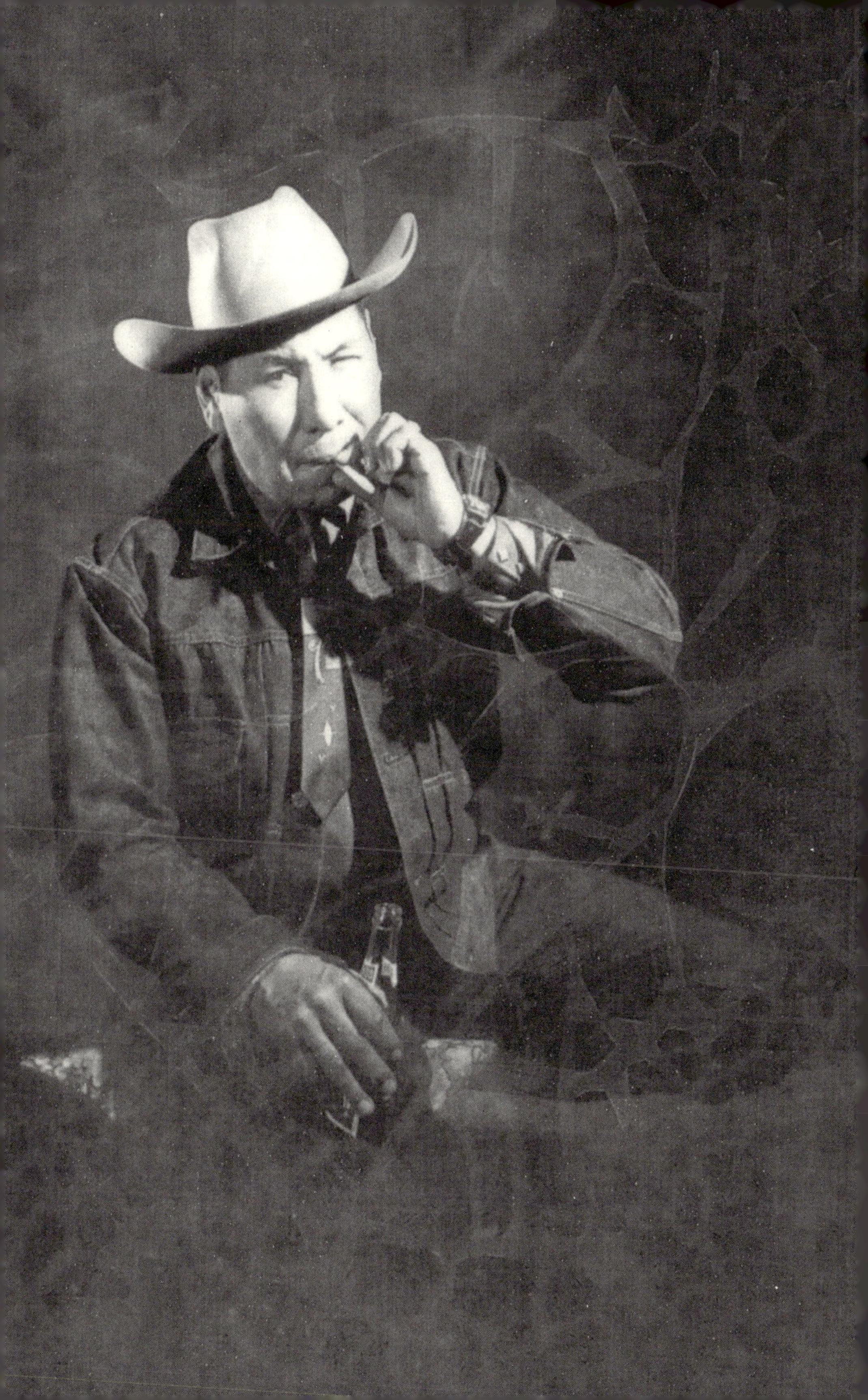

WEASEL TAIL

BATTLE WITH SOME CREES

MIKE ROSS RECORDED THE FOLLOWING ON 3 APRIL 1996. THE OLD MAN SPOKE BLACKFOOT. JOSEPHINE AND REG CROWSHOE WERE ALSO PRESENT. REG CROWSHOE BEGAN THE TRANSLATION IN JUNE 1996 AND JIMMY STRIKES WITH A GUN COMPLETED IT IN DECEMBER 1999; THE FOLLOWING COMBINES THE TWO.

Also translated as Chief Butcher or Stooping Over Butcher, Stokinota was Chief of the Peigans from 1901 to 1921. "As a boy his name was changed from Chief Straight Hair to Leans Over Butchering in recognition of one of his first acts of bravery" (Brownstone, 1993: 69–70). The Old Man's story recounts that war exploit.

Poplar is near the Missouri River on the Fort Peck Indian Reservation where two tribal groups live, Sioux and Assiniboine. By "the south side" the Old Man means across the Canada-United States border or the "medicine line."

JOE: *Óki.* When Red Chief [Chief Red Top] from the Peigans went to war. His other name was Cutting An Animal With His Head Down. He had a round camp [Sun Dance] on the east by the Oldman River, east side of the reserve some place. That's where they used to gather. There was a Blackfoot Indian where Red Top was a little boy. His mother told him and his sister to go with the leader of this war party and stick close by him. And they started. Way over. You know that place Poplar, Montana, on the south side, Montana? They went some place in that direction, on the south side; Poplar, Montana. Some Crees from Poplar, Montana, verified this story. They stopped at a few places along the trail from where they started and ate whatever they took for lunch. And the leader, the Blackfoot Nehnamaakiopii [?], found this rock in the shape of a man and he broke the leg of this rock effigy.

JOSEPHINE: **Listen to this, Reg.**

JOE: He was looking at it. Then Red Top took the rock that looked like a man and he took its leg and put it back together. He tied it together and put it back on the ground. Then they started again. This is one of their adventures along the road. On their travels as

166

this war party they were having unexplained things happening to them.

They got to where they were going. Up in the high hills of the place they were at the young warriors went ahead first. They saw the camps and the tipis of the enemy. Then they said to the Blackfoot leader that they were at the point where they were going to have the battle. Then Red Top and the other guy, the leader, went and sat on top of a hill. There were two of them.

Óki. They went down from those hills through the coulees. As they got closer to the camp the riders from the camp saw them. Red Top told his partner, "They've seen us." But the Blackfoot told him, "No, they haven't seen us." It wasn't too long, all of a sudden the riders came back. That was the enemy. Óki. At that point they had the battle and the rest of his men came down to help. He took off and kept looking back. He was running away.

JOSEPHINE: **Listen to this, Reg.**

JOE: **As he was running into a dry river bed, he tripped. He crawled into this grass when he fell, crawled under a bank where the grass grew over the edge. He crawled into that area and hid. He said, "All I heard were gunshots (they had guns at that time) and people fighting. That's all I heard." That was Red Top, the one that hid.**

JOSEPHINE: **That was Nehnamaakiopi [?] [Blackfoot]?**

JOE: **Blackfoot.**

JOSEPHINE: **Oh, Niinaasoki [?] [Blackfoot].**

JOE: **One of his other partners was sitting on top of a high hill. He just kept looking at the battle. The Blackfoot that sat on the high hill knew** that his comrades were all wiped out. But Red Top was still hiding while the battle was still going. As the sun went down all of a sudden a rider rode over to where Red Top was hiding. And the Cree turned his horse around to the sun and he pointed and he said, "Óki. For my kids, so that nothing will happen to them because they were part of this battle, I'm offering this Blackfoot to the sun." Then he rode away. He could have killed him easily. And Red Top kept hiding.

When it was dark he came out and he started home. But his partner that was documenting the battle from the top of the hill had already started home. He thought everybody had died. Red Top started home after him. As he started home there were certain places where they'd made lean-tos so the Blackfoot recorder [the man who documented the battle] would stop at those places and eat some of the supplies they had left. Then he would travel on to the next location where they'd hid some of their stuff that they used for supplies. And all this time Red Top kept following him home. As he got to some of these places he noticed some of the stuff was already eaten by the Blackfoot recorder.

One night as Red Top came close to home he stopped at one of the lean-tos that had supplies. As he sat there all of a sudden he saw these cranes flying towards him. He can hear them, the way they make sounds. [The Old Man makes bird sounds.] It was just about in the evening and all of a sudden he saw them fly past him, close by.

The Old Man's father's half-brother, Rides-at-the-Door, one of American anthropologist John C. Ewers's field informants, told Ewers about the type of lean-to referred to here. They were used when a raiding party was small or in a great hurry, one or two days away from enemy camps: "[A] simple double lean-to ... was made by leaning two sets of poles from opposite directions against a nearly horizontal out-stretched limb of a strong tree and covering the outside with bark. A triangular-shaped interior resulted" (Ewers, 1968: 121).

JOSEPHINE: **Listen to this.**

JOE: That's when he knew those were his comrades that got beaten at the battle; they were starting to go home. So he got up and he started following them, trying to get home. The Blackfoot recorder was ahead of him all this time. Red Top was still following behind, but he knew that the birds that had already flown by him were the spirits of his comrades.

JOSEPHINE: The ones that were dead, that were killed.

JOE: Red Top was sitting there, and he saw those birds when they flew by and he heard them making sounds. But they had human heads. As they flew by, as each one flew by, he saw they had human heads, each one like the head of one of his comrades. That's how he came to the conclusion that his comrades were coming home.

As the Blackfoot recorder got home first, he told his people that there were no survivors of all the comrades he went with to this battle. There were no survivors.

As Red Top sat on top of a high hill looking back at his own camp he was scared to go home. All of a sudden he saw one of the riders from camp ride by him while he was sitting there. He waved the rider over to him and the rider came up to see who he was. As the rider got close he used sign language and Blackfoot to communicate, to say, "Who's camp is this?" And the rider told him, "This is a Blackfoot camp. If you're speaking Blackfoot you're home already." He came off the hill and the rider advised him where his relatives were camped, which part of the circle. Right where Lone Fighters camped, that's where he went.

Members of each band, such as the Lone Fighters, customarily pitch their tipis together in assigned sections of a summer circle-camp. A band is typically made up of members of more than one clan. Anthropologists define Blackfoot-speakers' clans as lineage groups related through the father's or mother's bloodlines and bands as political affiliations (Sybille Manneschmidt to Mike Ross, personal communication 2001). Reg Crowshoe translates Lone Fighters (*Nitaitskaiks*) as "fight among themselves." Paul Raczka illustrates the circle-camp locations of the six recognized bands in "Winter Count" (Raczka, 1979: 11). The illustration caption omits the Blood or Bullrush people.

People started announcing through camp that Red Top had come home. They were all preparing a celebration, preparing to meet him. The Blackfoot recorder who got home first came back and told the Lone Fighters, "I didn't see him survive. I thought they were all killed and that's why I said there were no survivors." He told Red Top that evening when he met him at his camp, "I didn't know that you survived." Red Top invited him to stay in his camp until morning. In the morning his relatives came out and said, "Some time in the morning, Red Top is going to come out and tell the story of his survival." And the people started gathering together.

Chief Butcher, also known as Red Top, in front with the driver Malcolm McKenzie, and Big Plume in back, probably on the Peigan Reserve in 1912 (Glenbow Archives, NA 495-3).

Óki. In the morning Red Top went to the centre of the Sun Dance Lodge and he made smudge. As you know, Indian people don't forget smudge. He made smudge and he started talking about his story from the point where they started, the things that happened, the battle, how he survived, and his return trip home. Up to there is where I can tell the story.

WOLF TRAVELLER'S DEATH

MIKE ROSS RECORDED THE OLD MAN IN BLACKFOOT ON 3 APRIL 1996. REG CROWSHOE TRANSLATED IN JUNE 1996.

JOE: I knew this Old Man, Apisomakau, Wolf Traveller. He died on the south part of Brocket. I was a little boy then. I was riding around on horseback. My mother and father were camped here. And this month, 24 May, when the rodeo starts in Cowley, we all moved to Cowley. He was gathering up his horses and preparing to move to Cowley, chasing his horses around. He was sweating. He caught pneumonia and got sick. He went home, his place was across the river. We went to the rodeo.

Apisomakau, a son of Brings Down the Sun (Running Wolf), was the Old Man's maternal great-uncle. Brings Down the Sun's family tree is shown in McClintock (1968: 532), although the Old Man cautioned against relying solely on this type of possibly inaccurate information (see Joe Crowshoe interview, 23 May 1996).

When we got back, they said the Old Man is really sick. I went over and sat beside him as long as I could. He told me, "*Tsíki* [Young man], ride my horse. Ride over to the Timber [Limits] and tell Four Horns to come so that he can doctor me." It was a real nice strong horse, a bay with a blaze. The Old Man rode that horse. Nobody else rode it but my dad. About four o'clock that day I caught the horse, saddled it up, got on, and started. Today, these young people they just get into a vehicle and drive away. I got on the horse and I rode. I rode down to the Oldman River.

I went through high bush and across the river. I crossed it. I saw a coyote. It was barking at me. That was a bad sign. But I made it to Four Horns's camp. It was dark when I got there. I went over to where Four Horns was. They were getting ready for bed. They'd just finished chopping trees for posts and rails. I told him, "I was sent here as a messenger to tell you to break camp tomorrow to go doctor Wolf Traveller. He's really sick. Come back and heal him." He told me, "Sleep here in my camp." I told him, "I must start back." Four Horns said, "No. It's dark." But I refused to stay. I left. I went back out of camp and got on the horse and started home. As I started home, I heard the Dayliner [train] pass. It was six o'clock in the morning. I didn't want to ride the horse too hard. He was too precious. So I had to travel slow all night. When I got home I went into his camp and told him, "In the morning Four Horns is going to come."

Later that morning Four Horns and his family came and they started healing Wolf Traveller. Four Horns came and started doctoring him and I was doing the singing. He smudged the Old Man. The Old Man, Wolf Traveller, was a powerful Old Man. This is his song. [The Old Man sings.] And he used his eagle-bone whistle. He really liked his smoking, and he gave me his whistle and his drums. The Old Man got really sick as it came close to morning. That evening he started dressing up. It was a buckskin outfit with long fringes. The Old Man gave me that outfit. I used to use it when I used to camp at the Stampede. That's the outfit Wolf Traveller gave me at that time. And then the Old Man, Wolf Traveller, told me, "I'm gonna go away, I'm gonna go away." And as he falls asleep, Four Horns would cure him again and he would wake up.

All evening he was sleeping and Four Horns would sing his song and smudge him again and he would wake up again. Not long after, he gets doctored again—all evening until about twelve o'clock at night. The Old Man passed away around midnight. They were singing his song. They took his pipe, and they filled it with tobacco and they would take a puff of smoke from his pipe and blow it in his face. All of a sudden Wolf Traveller's eyes would move. About four o'clock in the morning, his eyes opened and he sat up. He said, "I can't see with my eyes. I need somebody to wipe them clean." They took some water and a cloth and wiped his eyes clean because he couldn't see good.

Wolf Traveller said to try hard: "The earth we live on is a hard place to live. I went for a while to a place where I felt good. It was a very good place. I ran east. My shadow left my body and I started running east. I walked into houses without even using doors. I saw people doing things. Old Man Red Paint never saw me. I was standing by him. There were some people looking at some papers. I was standing right beside them. They couldn't see me. That was Willy Big Bull and his wife.

Peigan Holy Woman and others at Sun Dance, Brocket, c.1940s. L. TO R.: ?, Mrs. Crow Flag, Mrs. Many Guns (wearing the *Naatoas* plumed headdress as Holy Woman), Many Guns, and Four Horns. (Glenbow Archives, NA 2045-14)

When I went by Pat Bad Eagle's, just east of his house, I heard my whistle and my drum. I tried to come back, but I couldn't. The wind was blowing from the west. So I started running back, zigzagging back and forth. When I got to the house I was looking through the window, looking at you guys. You were all crying. My body was laying there. And I came into the camp. I came in through my feet and I got back into my body. I smelt my smoke. Somebody was blowing it in my face. So I came to again. I felt like a plume, so light I just blew away."

And they said, "Tomorrow if the sun goes past noon you'll be okay."

So the next morning everybody was watching over him. I was sitting with them and Wolf Traveller told me, "I give you this song." I didn't believe him. At noon he laid down and he died. We brought him to the school. They had a church service and the next day he was buried. We left and went back to Wolf Flats, broke camp, and moved to Brocket where we live now. [The Old Man left the kitchen and returned with his eagle-bone whistle.]

The piercing Sun Dancers are the only ones who are given the eagle-bone whistle. Their faces are painted and the plume is put on the whistle. [He blows the whistle a few times.] In South Dakota, a boy from Browning, Montana, used my whistle. Grey Owl, or White Owl, fixed my whistle for me.

Seven

ℬROCKET

23 May 1996

MIKE ROSS RECORDED THE FOLLOWING IN BLACKFOOT ON 23 MAY 1996. THE OLD LADY AND REG CROWSHOE WERE ALSO PRESENT. REG TRANSLATED ON 27 AUGUST 1996.

SUN DANCES

JOE: *Óki*. The *Naatoas* [Sun Dance bundle] was given to me in July 1934. My grandmother, Long Hair, is who I had the Sun Dance with. I was gonna go to a rodeo in Yorkton, Saskatchewan. I was gonna go down with Guy Weadick, Tom Three Persons, and Pat Bad Eagle; four of us were gonna go down. I was gonna go with them, go by train and haul the horses down. I was going to look after the horses in the train, feeding them all the way to Yorkton. At the time we were ready to start I was captured to have a Sun Dance with my grandmother.

Guy Weadick (1886–1953) was an American vaudeville and rodeo performer who, with four financial backers, staged the first Calgary Exhibition and Stampede in 1912 (Glenbow Archives, Guy Weadick fonds). Tom Three Persons (1885–1948), a Blood, competed at that first Calgary Stampede where he rode "the notorious outlaw horse Cyclone to a standstill in front of a packed closing day grandstand to win the bronc riding championship" (Gray, 1985: 38).

> The Old Man's maternal grandmother, Long Hair, chose, or captured, him because a woman who vows to give a Sun Dance needs a male partner: "Should this woman be a single woman she would have to get some of her brothers or uncles or cusins [sic] to be her man, partner, during her medicine lodge ceremony. But she would not get any body outside of her own kin folks" (New Breast quoted in Duvall's uncorrected field notes as cited in Manneschmidt and Crowshoe, 1997: 32).

They brought me out early in the morning. My friend, Jim Wells, also came. He told me, "My partner, we're going down to Yorkton to the rodeo. We're gonna work in the arena and open the chutes for the cowboys when they're ready to come out. We'll also ride because we'll get one dollar a mount for every horse we ride."

JOSEPHINE: **One dollar!**

JOE: And then I didn't go. I was brought to the Sun Dance and that's where I stayed for four days not eating or drinking.

Sun Dance on the Peigan Reserve in the 1920s. (Glenbow Archives, PA 3280-2)

JOSEPHINE: It's really hard. I know. When you have to fast, you don't eat and you don't drink; you just pray. At the Sun Dance you just pray all the time, "sit holy." Then the Great Spirit can hear you good when you do that.

JOE: *Óki.* That's why I'm saying that our Indian ways are strong, holy things. Now this Horse Sun Dance. There is one Sun Dance called "Horse Sun Dance." Listen, across the river, tipis were blowing over and that was where they were gonna have the Sun Dance. Then people moved down towards the river. And that's where they had the Sun Dance. I don't know who was the guy that had the Sun Dance for the Horse Sun Dance. It's been a long time. That was the time that Josephine's mother [Lucy Warrior] was born at the Horse Sun Dance [c.1894].

JOSEPHINE: That was the time my mother was born.

Josephine Crowshoe's mother, Lucy Yellowhorn (born c.1894), married Sam Warrior (born c.1891). She had two stepsons, Sam, or Bernard, Bastien (c.1908) and George Bastien (c.1912) and four children with Sam: Josephine (c.1917), Pete (c.1919), Henry (c.1922), and Edward (1924). Josephine's family's birth dates are from the 1923 treaty payment list held in Glenbow Archives (Glenbow Archives, Indian Agency fonds M1826 f11).

JOE: That was the time when the Peigan Reserve had a lot of horses. [In] all the transfers at the Sun Dance, horses were being paid — horse after horse after horse.

JOSEPHINE: Yeah, that's why it's called *ponokaomitaa Ookáán.*

REG: Each year is recorded by the Sun Dances.

JOSEPHINE: Yeah, some do that but not all really, no.

JOE: Look, I had the Sun Dance [with] my grandmother, Long Hair. She said, "My daughter's sick right now. My daughter's really sick. This summer I'm going to have a Sun Dance so she will get better." That summer she went ahead and had the Sun Dance. They said, "We've got no man to have a Sun Dance with her." At that point I was pointed out to have the Sun Dance with my grandmother. I went ahead and had the Sun Dance with her. That's when she gave me the *Naatoas*, headdress bundle.

JOSEPHINE: That's when he owned that bundle.

JOE: This person by the name of Ki'sómm, he was the guy that sang at the ceremonies. He was a good singer. That guy is the reason I know all the Sun Dance songs. His name was Ki'sómm. This person from the Bloods, his name was Chief Moon. I think those were his relatives, the Chief Moons. When the centre pole came up and we quit and I went to have the sweat, I became ill. They put me on a blanket and they lifted me and brought me home.

> Adolf Hungry Wolf writes that Ki'sómm, or, as he spells it, Ki-soum, was "a holy man, a doctor, and a minor chief as head of the Fish Eaters band" (Hungry Wolf, 1977: 55).

JOSEPHINE: That's what happened to him because he never ate. He had to fast for four days.

JOE: There are a lot of other Sun Dances that I know. When I was a young boy I had to watch over a lot of horses. I had to take them for water in the evening and in the morning. People chased horses in. We had to go and help them push them into camp. There was a lot of horses in camp [laughs].

REG: [To Mike in English] And they were running horses into each other when he was young, when they were chasing horses back and forth from the Sun Dance to water. One group will be coming and he'll drive

Blackfeet ceremonialist Charlie Reevis (Sooie) from Browning, Montana, leading the Holy Woman (fifth in line) during a 1930s Sun Dance held on the Blood Reserve (Káínaa). Unknown photographer. (Glenbow Archives, NA 667-1011)

his group head on into the other one. As young people they were doing crazy things.

JOSEPHINE: He's talking about when he was a little boy that he did things that he shouldn't do. [The Old Man laughs] He was saying at the Sun Dance, they go water the horses and sometimes he'd be there driving these horses back and somebody else would be driving their horses to the water and they bump. [Laughter] But the horses would know where to go. They don't go crazy and go back. They know where they're going, yeah.

JOE: Back in my youth there were a lot of horses. We had horse races out on the prairie during Sun Dances. We always had races and rodeos.

Look here, you and me [looking to his wife], we started our Sun Dance. We went to Evelyn and Bruce [a daughter and son-in-law]. They were living in Kelowna [British Columbia]. That's where we went to visit about two years before. When we got there Evelyn told us, "I had a dream. I'm going to tell you my dream." She said, "I dreamt that I was walking up from down east and this man told me, 'Here comes your mother and father, they're walking this way. Tell them this summer to have a Sun Dance.'" And that's what she told me. That's why I went ahead and had our Sun Dance in 1977; 1977 is when we had our Sun Dance over at Lizard's house just over to the prairie side. That's when I started working with Mike Swims Under the first time, in 1977. Look, I gave him a tipi and a tent and a camp stove. All that to take home.

JOSEPHINE: New camp stove and a tent for helping the Old Man. That's how they trade things. You know, Indians, you don't buy. Give me this much for this, dollars. You, me, no. You give me goods. What I need. That's what I want. That's the way Indians trade. They call it trade. They don't call [it] buy.

Seven

Photographed by T. George Anderton at a Sun Dance near Fort Macleod, c.1886. The riders may be warning against taking photographs, forbidden at many ceremonies. (Provincial Archives of Alberta, A18696)

Thomas George Naylor Anderton (c.1848–1895) born in Leeds, England, emigrated to Montreal, Quebec, joined the North West Mounted Police in 1876, and served at Fort Walsh in what became southwestern Saskatchewan. He took his discharge at Fort Macleod in 1879 and became one of Alberta's first commercial photographers, operating studios in partnership, and on his own, in Medicine Hat, Fort Macleod, and Lethbridge. He was also a brewer and saloon-keeper. His few remaining photographs of Sioux, Blackfoot, Peigan, Blood, Cree, Assiniboine, and NWMP subjects of the 1870s and 1880s are in Glenbow's collections (*Alberta History* 25: 4 [Autumn 1977]: 17–24; see also file on "Photographers" in Glenbow Archives).

BOTTLE AND FEATHER

MIKE ROSS RECORDED THE FOLLOWING IN BLACKFOOT ON 23 MAY 1996. REG CROWSHOE TRANSLATED ON 27 AUGUST 1996.

JOE: This Old Man went to get rations. When he was on his way home from getting rations he found a bottle and an eagle feather. He arrived at the new agency in Brocket, which was a long haul. At that time I used to be interpreter. He said, "There's a government official who's here now who wants us to stop our ceremonies and dances. He says, 'All you're doing is giving each other sicknesses.'" The Old Man [Nap Big Bull] was sitting there. When they were finished he said to them, "Óki. I will speak now, the floor is mine." The Old Man prayed. He told the government official, "I won't take long." He took the bottle and then he took the feather. "Take one of these. You came from the government to stop us from doing our Indian way."

The white man sat there for a long time, thinking, then asked, "What is it? What is it?"

Big Bull replied, "[Now] you take whichever one you want." The white man got up, picked up the whiskey bottle and sat back down. Big Bull told him, "Alcohol belongs to the white man. Now you've taken it back. We will take our feather and we will keep it and we will watch the eagle flying up in the sky for a long, long time. We're not going to stop our holy ways. You all saw that the white man took the whiskey bottle. It doesn't take a dollar a long time to be spent. That's what alcohol is. It is very bad." Then the Old Man said to go back, straight down east, and tell people where he came from the way he saw things and the way things are out west. The white man left to the government to advise them of what was going on. It wasn't long after the government replied back to the native people that they could continue their ceremonies.

Seven

Big Bull in the morning was going to start his pipe dance. Big Bull told the agent, "Tomorrow I'm going to have my medicine pipe dance." They told Mr. Brown [?], "Don't open your Pipe, they're going to arrest you." Nap Big Bull set up a tipi anyway. He went to the agency and told the agent, "The food is ready, the payments are ready, the ceremonialists are ready, I'm just going to go ahead and start. I'm not going to stop. If you want to stop me, you're going to have to come to my house and pick me up." So, he went back home and started the ceremony and waited for the agent to come. It was only a mile away but the agent never showed up. When the ceremony was over he went back to the agent and told the agent, "We are finished now. You can arrest me now." That it is why today, for myself, I try really hard to smudge and keep the Indian way going. It is so important.

This story probably took place in the 1930s because "that's when Nap Big Bull had the bundle" (Reg Crowshoe to Mike Ross, personal communication 1996). "Nap" is short for Napoleon.

JOSEPHINE: [Speaking English] You know what my grandmother told me? I still think of it today and I still go by it. She told me [speaking in a strong voice], "We believe that God made all the people, the Indian People. He gave them all a religion." *Náápiikoaiksi*, this one is sitting here, the white people, He gave them religion. Still go by it. He gave us our way, He gave the Black people their way. Different nationalities, He gave them, and we don't laugh at *náápiikoan*'s way. [Speaking softly,] I was raised at *náápiikoan*'s way, believing it. I believe. And I believe my Indian way, my Indian religion. I believe it and I don't laugh at the Black people when they pray. I don't laugh because it's a God-given thing.

183

WEASEL TAIL

Peigan congregation at St. Peter's Anglican mission, c.1900. Nap Big Bull is standing back row, third from right; all others unidentified. Several people in the photograph wear white shell earrings. (Glenbow Archives, NA 1020-36)

"Medicine Pipe Owners and their families used to wear these symbols all the time. Now most people wear them [earrings, bracelets, and necklaces] only to ceremonies. They serve as a constant reminder of the main elements of nature: shells to represent water; blue beads to represent the sky; thongs to represent animals; and a coating of sacred red paint to represent Earth" (Hungry Wolf, 1977: 133).

WHERE TO PRAY

MIKE ROSS RECORDED THE OLD MAN IN BLACKFOOT ON 23 MAY 1996. JOSEPHINE AND REG CROWSHOE WERE ALSO PRESENT. JIMMY STRIKES WITH A GUN TRANSLATED IN DECEMBER 1999.

JOE: A long time ago when the missionaries and priests came, the priests would tell the people, "When you die you go to Heaven, if you pray." So they built a church and there were two friends and one guy told his friend, "Take your pipe and we'll go to church." The church was where the old agency was across the river. They heard the bell when they were ringing the bell, so he told his friend, "Take your pipe and your pipe bag and we'll go." People started arriving at the church. And the priest told them, "This is where we're gonna pray on Sundays."

The Old Man said, "It's really good we can pray inside. Where I pray is outside, out in the open." And he told his friend, "Light your pipe so we can smoke it."

The priest told him, "No, you can't."

The Old Man told the priest, "I thought you said this is where we pray? Me and my friend came here to pray, now you're chasing us out." The reason why they got chased out? When the church service started the two Indians lit their pipe and started praying in their language. They were trying to out-do the priest. So the priest chased them out. So the Old Man and his friend said, "Gee, this is a church. I thought the priest said we'll be going to Heaven when we pray."

When people die they go to Heaven. St. Peter was by the door. When they get there St. Peter would look at their papers and St. Peter would say, "This is how much you give me before you go into Heaven." One day an Indian and a coloured guy went up there to St. Peter. St. Peter told the Indian, "I don't see your name here. You give me twenty-five dollars, then you can come in." So the Indian went back down and the coloured guy went down too. He died and he went up again. St. Peter asked the coloured guy, "Where's the Indian?"

And the coloured guy replied, "Oh, he's down there trying to borrow some money. He's gone to the bank and he's trying to get a co-signer!"

TIPI TRANSFERS

MIKE ROSS RECORDED THE OLD MAN ON TIPI TRANSFERS ON 23 MAY 1996. HE SPOKE BLACKFOOT. JOSEPHINE AND REG CROWSHOE WERE ALSO PRESENT. REG TRANSLATED ON 27 AUGUST 1996.

JOE: *Óki*. I gave the Four Buffalo Hoof design to Reg in Calgary. Two years ago I gave it to him and he paid good on it. Today, the Four Buffalo Hoof design is from here, it's Peigan's design. The Race Horse Society presented a pipe to get the Four Buffalo Hoof design at a Sun Dance on the reserve. I know it. Philip Big Swan is who they went after for the tipi. Philip said, "No. It's not my home, [it's] Big Swan's father's tipi." Then he told Old Man Big Swan, "The Race Horse Society have approached me for this design, given me a pipe." Man Who Smokes was an older adviser to the Race Horse Society. Those are the advisers—my dad, Charlie Grier, there were a lot of them, Jim Little Leaf. They were part of the Race Horse Society. They all put their goods together, their money, and that tipi was transferred to them. And the Old Man, they put the goods beside him. Then they took the tipi and the tipi was given to Man Who Smokes.

The Society told Man Who Smokes, "Here's the tipi. Hold it in trust for us so when we're gonna use it, we'll take it." Then that winter, Man Who Smokes got sick. He told my dad, "Take the tipi and hold it."

The Race Horse Society had a meeting and my dad told them, "Man Who Smokes told me he's sick. Now he's told us to take our tipi."

And then the members said, "Well, he's been looking after it. Leave it at his place." So, Man Who Smokes maintained to hold it.

Then my dad went back to Man Who Smokes and told him, "You're told to hold it."

And Man Who Smokes said, "It's not going to be long before I die." Charlie Davis, a Blood Indian, also came at that time and was told by Man Who Smokes, "I've got Race Horse Society's home, the Four Buffalo

Hoof design. Hold it for them. When they need it they can come and get it." And Charlie Davis, his name in Blackfoot means Doesn't Cook, he took it home to the Bloods. There was a shield that went with it.

I owned the Elk design tipi. My dad sold it. He gave it to Pat Plain Eagle. Many Chiefs was the one that came after it. He gave it to him. There was a dance. There was an honour dance for Pat Plain Eagle at that dance that fall. At his honour dance, he gave it to George First Rider, Blood Indian. George took the tipi and he went home. In the summer I saw it over at the Bloods, at the Sun Dance. When I go there and I look at it, I say, "This is my tipi." Now there are a lot of people that are saying, "I own the Elk design." There are a lot of claims to it.

JOSEPHINE: **Listen to this, Reg.**

JOE: I gave about twelve head of horses to the Blackfoot man from the north. In those days, there were a lot of horses. My relative Long Hair [maternal grandmother], Sun Dance Cane Woman [maternal great-aunt], and other old ladies, they all had a lot of horses. So, I went to chase in twelve head and that's what I paid for that tipi. I gave them to that man from North Blackfoot [Fox Head].

Listen here, nowadays these things they argue about, these young people don't know. They all don't know. This Elijah Harper from Manitoba said not too long ago, "Our young people today are bringing our holy ways in all kinds of directions. They say things they don't know what they're talking about."

Elijah Harper was born on the Red Sucker Lake First Nation (Cree), Manitoba. He was Band Chief there and later won a seat in the Manitoba legislature. He became well known for his role in blocking approval of the 1990 Canadian Meech Lake Accord, which proposed transferring powers from the central federal government to the provinces, giving the largely francophone province of Quebec recognition as a "distinct society" as well as the right to veto future constitutional

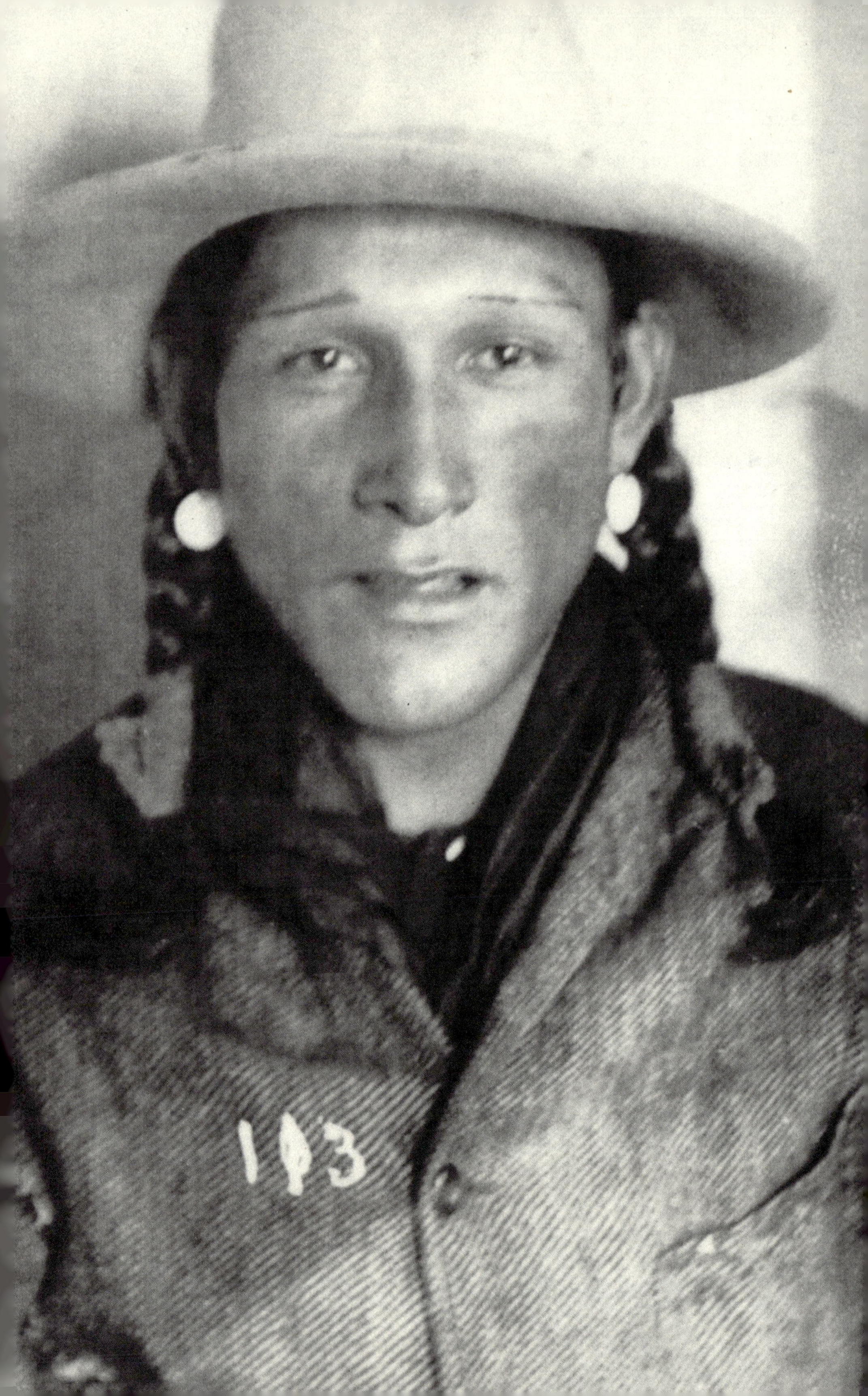
143

changes. Harper formally indicated his rejection by holding up an eagle feather during the vote in the Manitoba Legislature. He resigned his seat and became an MP in the Canadian government (http://en.wikipedia.org/wiki/Elijah_Harper).

JOSEPHINE: That's right. But there's some that do that. There's some that are going the right way.

JOE: Look, summer, my mother told me, "Look at all these tipis. The one you like we'll go present the pipe." Jimmy Wells and myself we started going to tipis I liked around the camp. When we got to ones I liked, the people were gone or weren't home. A lot of people were driving away. I got back home. My mother asked me, "Did you find anything that you liked among these tipis?"

And I said, "No. There's nobody home in these tipis."

The Old Lady said, "Come over here." So I went out of the tipi with her. She said, "Right here is the Four Buffalo Hoof design tipi. Peigan. Your father was part of the Race Horse Society and that was their home. Why don't you go over and present the pipe to that lodge."

So I went over there and Rides-at-the-Door, he limps, he came over and told me, "Dog is the one that's using that tipi. He's living in there." Percy Creighton, he was the one living in there at the time.

The next day in the evening the Old Man prepared a pipe for me and he put it there. The next morning he told me to take it to the Four Buffalo Hoof Lodge tipi and go in and give it to the owner. Tell him, "Your home," and point to the design, "give it to me."

JOSEPHINE: That's the way they used to do it.

On opposite page: Charlie Davis, Kainaa (Blood), 23 August 1906, age twenty-five, arrested for horse stealing, at NWMP Fort Macleod. Doesn't Cook was another name for Charlie Davis. Some fashionable young men like him plucked their eyebrows (Fitz-Gibbon, 1985: 26). (Glenbow Archives, NA 258-17)

WEASEL TAIL

The Old Man's mother, Everybody Listens To, Ekistinopa, with granddaughters. Photograph by Gordon Crighton, 3 March 1958. (Glenbow Archives, NB 44-59f)

The Old Man's mother, known after her second marriage as Laura Buffalo, Brocket 1969. (Courtesy Royal Alberta Museum)

JOE: Anyway, the next morning my mother took blankets and money and followed me over to the Four Buffalo Hoof design. Percy Creighton was already up and I sat down beside him. I gave him the pipe and he looked at me and said, "What?"

And I said, "Give me your home here."

And he said, "Oh, wait, let me have some coffee." He got up. He said, "Right where my altar is, where I make my smudge, put that loaded pipe there." So I put it there. He told me, "Come over and sit here." So I went over and I sat there next to him. Then he told me, he said, "I'm going to tell you this tipi lodge design is not my home. Doesn't Cook, it's his home." All he used to use this tipi for was to cover his grain when it was harvested. When it rains or there is inclement weather he uses this tipi for covering. One day I saw it. I went over there and I looked at the tipi and it was still in good shape.

And I told Charlie Davis, "This upcoming Sun Dance could you lend me this tipi?"

And then he [Percy Creighton] told me, "I went to chop tipi poles and then he [Doesn't Cook] gave me the tipi design. He loaned me the tipi and that's why I'm using it at this *Ookáán*. That's the guy that owns this tipi. Right now I'm going to saddle up my horse, I picketed it next to the tipi. I'm going to ride over to his house. He's working on his farm. He's just about home. I'll talk to him."

I watched out for him in camp. All of a sudden I saw him come back and I went over to meet him, and then he told me, "*Óki*." After he made smudge and prayed, he told me, "Pick up the pipe and light it," and I lit it. "When it lights up good give it to me." When it lit good, I gave it to him and he was smoking it. And then he told me, "*Óki*. You got a home."

Charlie Davis asked, "Who was the one that gave the pipe for this tipi design?" And I told him, "Deer Chief's son is the one that gave me the pipe for it."

Charlie Davis said, "Oh, just give it to him. I got nothing to say to it. Just give it to him."

JOSEPHINE: That's the proof.

JOE: At the time when we all moved away in different directions from the Sun Dance circle-camp, Percy Creighton brought over the tipi. In 1929, in August, that's when I got it. I had a good crop, a nice crop. And the man, Dog [Percy Creighton], he painted my face on the tipi. I gave him two horses, one sorrel and one bald-face. He took them home. Now I own that Four Buffalo Hoof design tipi in the right way.

JOSEPHINE: That's a good truth you have on there.

JOE: Look, it wasn't too long before it was really old. I went to buy canvas and you sewed it. I was drawing it and repainting it and we made a new one.

JOSEPHINE: Right, I remember that. It was really old. Then he bought a new material to paint the tipi. We did it all over again. It's new now.

REG: [In Blackfoot] What about the Snake Design tipi?

JOSEPHINE: [To the Old Man in Blackfoot] That was his tipi, the Old Man's father's.

JOE: I really don't know that much about the Snake Design tipi. The only one I know is the Snake Design from the Bloods. Don Shade owns it.

Top photo on opposite page: Traditionally, women owned the family tipi and were responsible for putting it up and taking it down, which they could do in less than an hour. Four tied-together poles make the frame of the Blackfoot-speaker's tipi; a dozen or more poles wedge into these and the last pole, raised at the back, has the heavy canvas tipi cover tied to it. From a 2 March 1958 sequence of photographs by Gordon Crighton. (Glenbow Archives, NB 44-58k)

Bottom photo on opposite page: The Four Buffalo Hoof design tipi cover is wrapped around the poles with the entrance facing east towards the rising sun, and the back against the strong west wind. The Old Man is on the right. (Glenbow Archives, NB 44-58m)

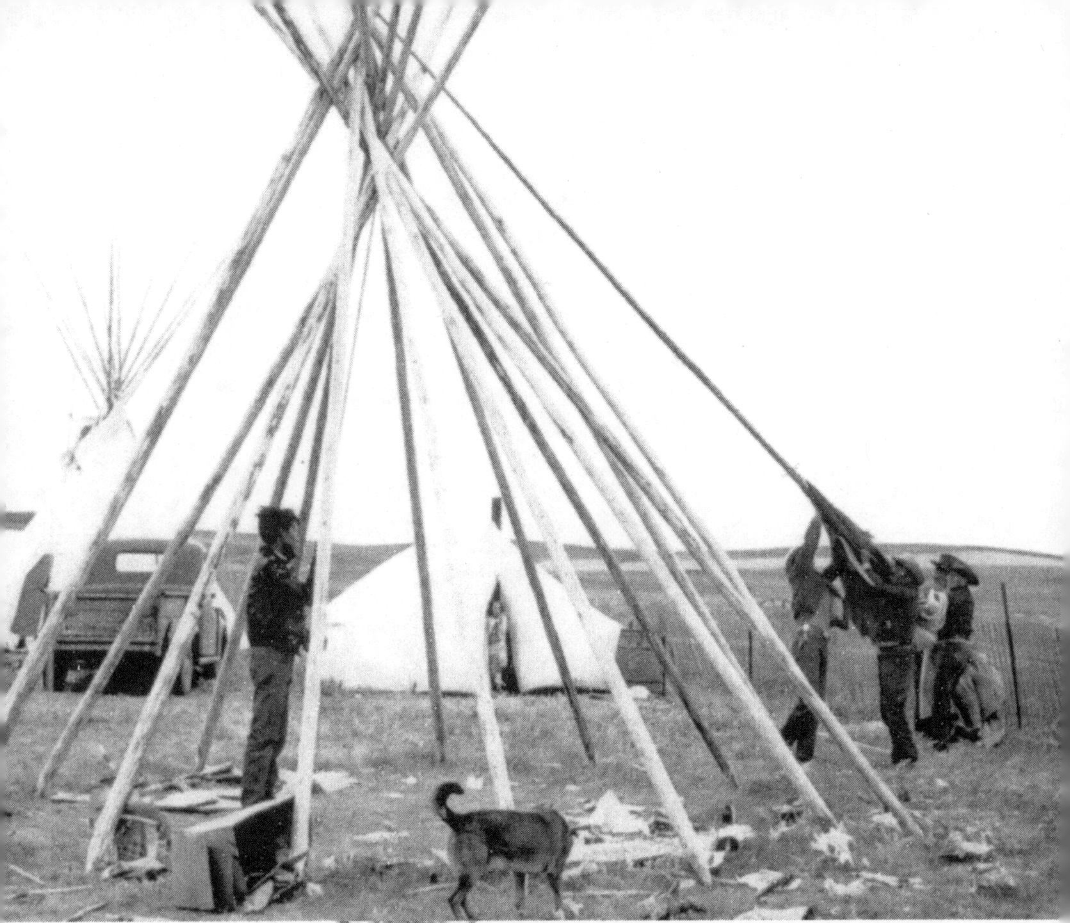

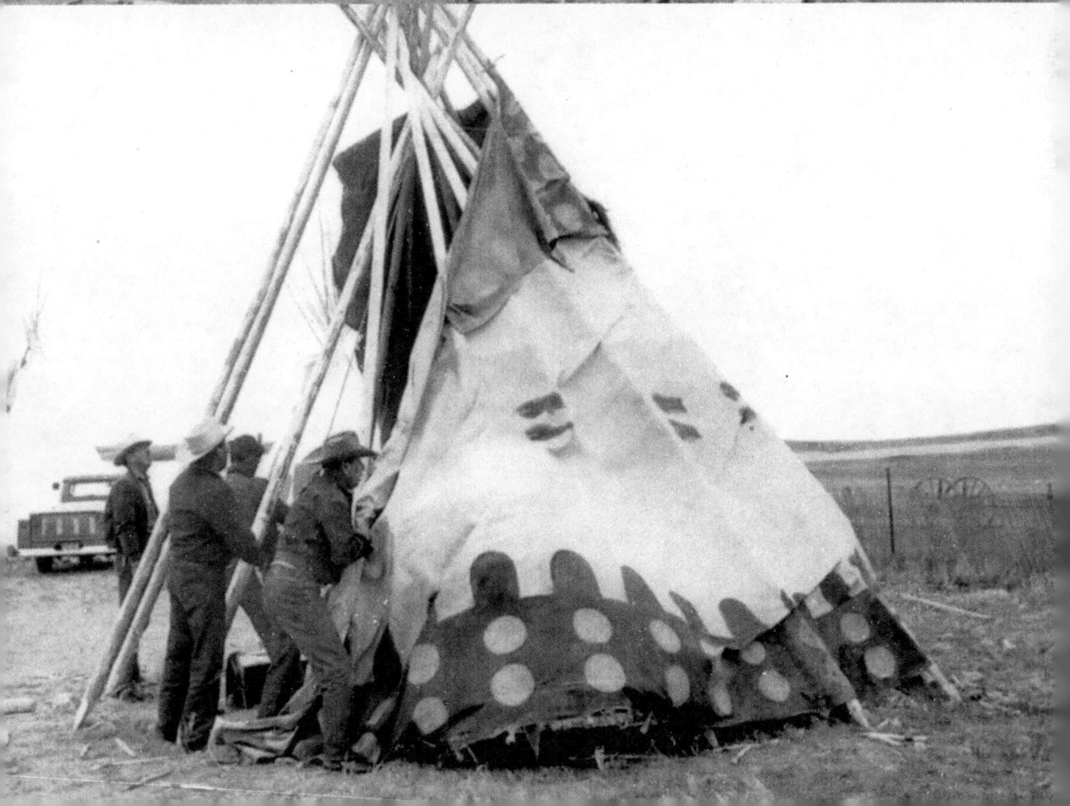

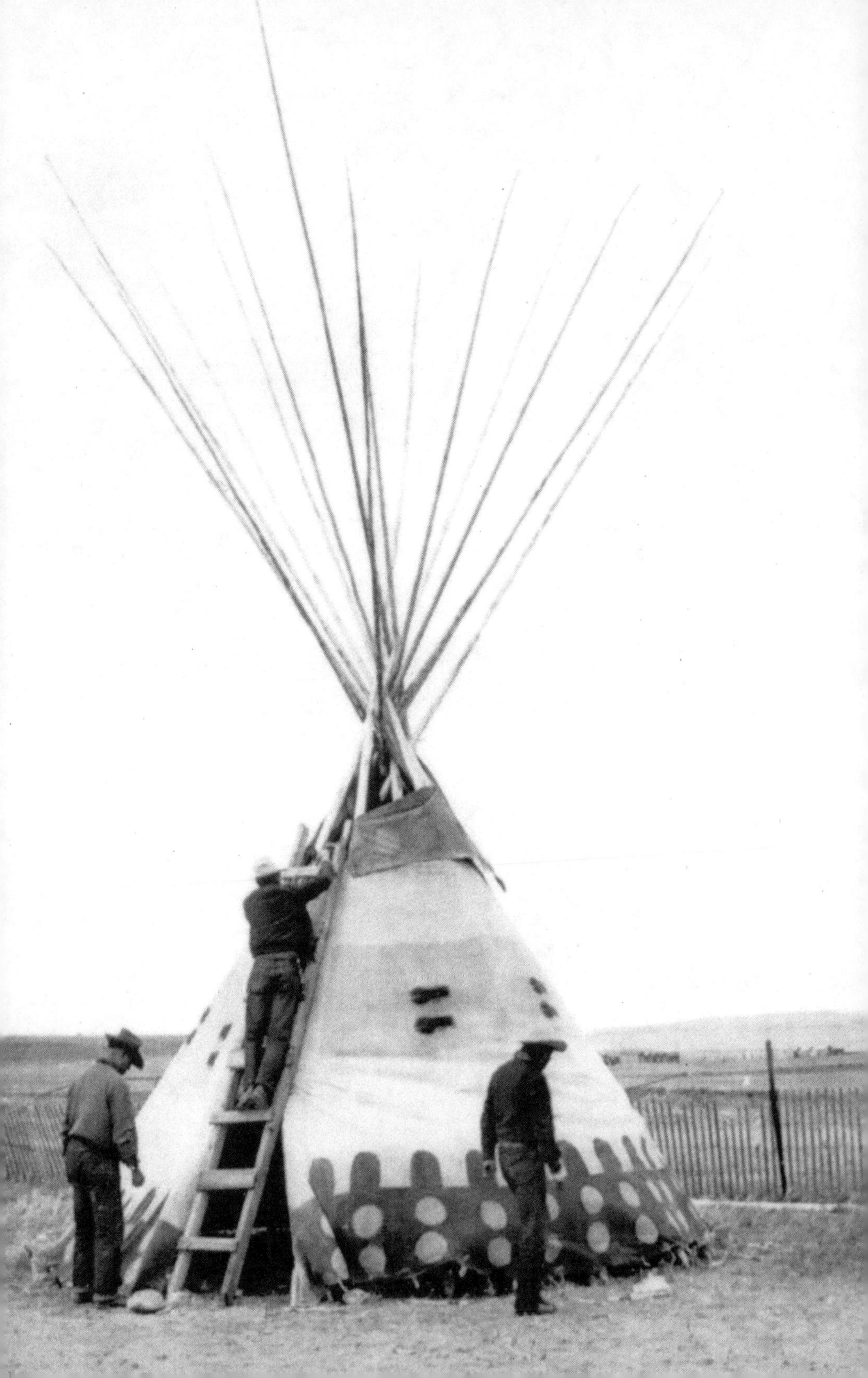

JOSEPHINE: Awakasina [the Old Man's father, Deer Chief] owned that design too. The Old Lady gave the Old Man [the Old Man's father] the Thunder Design tipi. Those are rightfully owned and rightfully passed on.

JOE: Now in Calgary everybody puts up their lodges. We should be checking on those tipis at the Calgary Stampede Indian Village to see which is legally theirs and which is legally not theirs. That should be checked on. And then they can talk about the paint, their transfers, designs, and then we'll know. That's a way of recording.

JOSEPHINE: Yeah. You do that Mike. He'll do it.

REG: He'll get thrown out of Indian Village in Calgary!

MIKE: I'll have to wear my running shoes!

JOSEPHINE: Never mind his laugh, just go ahead. I don't mind. I don't care if he laughs.

REG: He's going to wear his running shoes so he can run away!

JOE: Look, these tipis ... they're all dreams. The Red Old Man's tipi was called the Black Buffalo Lodge design. [Reg notes during translation that he was called that because he was covered with ochre.] He was sitting along the river. A couple of boys, they were looking at the river. And where there were clear spots all of a sudden they saw two tipis on the river bottom. They went over and looked into the water, and every time it becomes clear they see these two lodges in the water. One said, "I'll own that one," and the other said, "I'll own the other tipi design."

On opposite page: Wooden-stick buttons fasten the cover together and pickets pin it to the ground. Decorated cloth liners, attached part way up inside the tipi, keep out cold drafts. Two poles adjust ear flaps to vent smoke from the camp fire inside. (Glenbow Archives, NB 44-58n)

JOSEPHINE: You know, those are mysterious things but nobody *náápi-ikoan* would understand that.

JOE: There are a few tipis that I know: the Elk Lodge, the Buffalo Hoof Lodge, those are transferred tipis, and the Thunder design tipi and the Snake tipi, the one Heather [a granddaughter] owns.

REG: Do they still use the tipi transfer ceremony?

JOE: There are very few people today that can run a transfer. Between the Bloods, Peigan, and Gleichen [Blackfoot] there are very few people. I'm almost the only one who knows how and is still doing the transfers. Our transfers of tipi designs, those are the songs we'll sing in a tipi transfer. Those guys who are going to be using the rattles, singing the songs in the tipi transfer ceremony, those are also powerful people for them to know the songs. One is called the "All Tipi Song" and then there are other tipi songs. When you sing them at the tipi transfer, you're giving them to the person who's getting the tipi design transferred to him. The way you would get tipi designs would be to fill a pipe with tobacco and offer it to the owner.

JOSEPHINE: If he takes the pipe, she'll give you the tipi design. When I was young, in my days, I remember there's certain people that had designs come to them through dreams. And when they have a dream, they go talk to the Elder [to have the design ratified] and then they mark the design on a tipi.

Seven

Painted tipis, 1996. Designs, L. TO R.: "Where the Seven Brothers Lived," "Keep Our Circle Strong," "Four Buffalo Hoof," and "Snake." (© Gordon Petersen)

Eight

*B*ROCKET

27 October 1998

MIKE ROSS REMINDED THE OLD MAN OF SEVERAL STORIES HE HAD WANTED TO TELL ME. HE SPOKE MIXED BLACKFOOT AND ENGLISH. JIMMY STRIKES WITH A GUN TRANSLATED THE BLACKFOOT PORTIONS IN DECEMBER 1999.

AISSKO'KIINAIKSI: ANTS

JOE: [In Blackfoot] There was an old man out on the prairie. He was riding. He got off his horse and he was eating his lunch and he fell asleep. He had a dream. Creator told him, "Get up, you're laying by the ants."

JOSEPHINE: The ants, yeah.

JOE: *Óki.* So the man went home. When he got home that night he went to sleep. While he was asleep, a man came to him and told him, "Those ants you were looking at, they were all black. Many of them. They were all working. They are gonna become human, and they're gonna come here."

A time later his son told him, "Let's go see those new people that just arrived." He harnessed up the team and wagon and went over there.

His son told him, "They're selling potatoes and other plants." He realized that these people were Hutterites. Then he remembered his dream that he had. The man had told him in his dream that there was a new bunch of people that were going to come. The man was sitting there watching the Hutterites. All of them were working. The older people weren't working. They were looking after them. All ants are always working.

Hutterites are Anabaptist Christians first led by Jacob Hutter in the 1500s. They strictly adhere to New Testament Biblical teachings and live together in colonies holding all things in common. They moved to the United States (1878) and Canada (1918) from Austria and Russia, escaping religious persecution and because of their pacifism and war-resistance (Walman and Stahl, 1985; Hoffer, 1998; www.hutterites.org).

[In English] You see, this old man had a dream. He dreamt about ants. On the ground, on the ground [taps the table], ants, he seen them. Everybody's working, all those small ants working. When they can't, they help each other bring [things to] the old people inside, to the old people inside. This old man said, "I had a dream. Somebody told me, 'New kind a people coming, new people coming here. They gonna do the farming, they gonna work all over. Even the kids work.'" So his son went, went to the Hutterites. He bought potatoes, turnips, bread. He said, "I seen them before. They were ants. They wear black clothes all over. Black clothes." So that's the story of the ants. See, the ants they live underground. They work, they all over, collecting food for the old people down there [raps the table top]. And there's ants outside where I live. When I see them, I feed them sugar. They bring the sugar inside. All of them help one another. And the ants said, "Inside there's some old people who we're going to feed." And today my children come and they feed me.

On opposite page: Hutterite girls in southern Alberta, 1934. (Glenbow Archives. NA 5374-7)

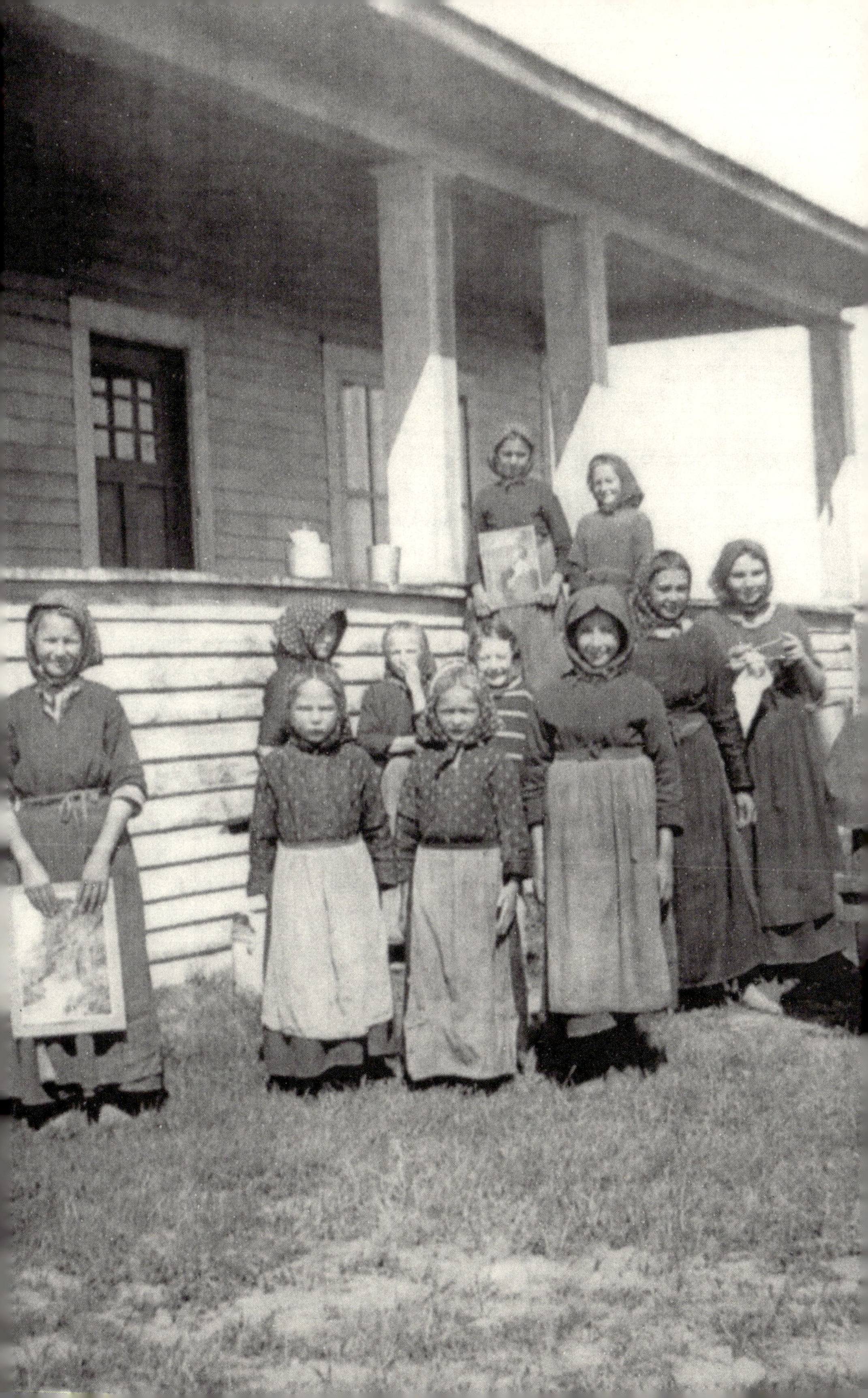

GHOST HOUSE

JOE: When Fort Macleod was first built there were two boys from the reserve who were out drinking in Fort Macleod. The police [NWMP] saw them, so they took off west along the Oldman River. They came upon this house where the people that died were kept. So one boy ran inside this house and saw a body that was laying there. So he laid beside it. The boy's name was Charlie Strikes With A Gun. When the police arrived they checked in the house. He was watching the police as the police were looking inside the house, but they couldn't find [him]. The officer called his partner and said, "They have to be in here." The police went outside and said, "Yeah, I saw him go in there, let's go check inside again." So they went back in. But when they went back in, the boy had sat up but the police didn't see him. So the policeman went back out and told his partner. Then his partner went in and he couldn't see him, couldn't find anybody in the house. After they left, the boy went outside, saw his horse, and he just got on the horse and left. He took off. It wasn't long after he died.

JOSEPHINE: [In English] That's really something. Did you know what he was talking about? He was talking about the police chasing these two guys [who were] drinking. And one of the guys went into this house where you put the dead people. There was a grave. It was all out. He just lay there beside this dead person and told him, "They're in to get me. I was watching the police. They came in, looked all around but they never seen me lying there. Then they left."

JOE: [In English] They didn't see him.

JOSEPHINE: You're a *náápiikoan*. Me, I'm Indian. You don't believe what I believe. You believe that? Nooo.

Prior to contact with whites, Plains peoples such as Peigans did not bury bodies but often placed them in tipis called "death lodges," left wrapped bodies above ground on free-standing or tree-built scaffolds, or placed them on rocky prominences and in crevices and coulees. They believed the dead person's spirit needed to be free. "Discounting Native concerns regarding the soul's ability to escape from the body, missionaries brought the European ideal of interment as part of their ambitious religious agenda" (Wilson, 1993: 75). Wooden structures, or "ghost houses," were a compromise between traditional mortuary customs and Christian ideals (Wissler and Duvall, 1995: xviii). "The [Blackfeet] ghost-house is a small rectangular wooden structure, averaging some seven feet wide and eleven to thirteen feet long. The construction is modeled after the early reservation cabin, with commercial boards replacing logs in the later sites" (Nuttall, 1960: 24). For this type of grave house see Skunk Tallow's grave in Glenbow photograph NA 883-1. The Old Man's story may refer to this type of burial structure.

THE HAUNTED BRACELETS

JOE: *Óki.* At the old agency down there, there was a stockman. He was a white guy, looked after the cattle. One day he told the boys, "You Indians are superstitious. You're scared of ghosts. There're no ghosts." When the boys were working they came across a burial site on a hill. So they sat down and were eating their lunch. One boy was sitting by the white man and he told him, "Take these bracelets." And the white man took the bracelets and put them in his pocket. The boy told him, "[A ghost is] gonna come and get the bracelets."

The "white guy" was William Betts, though the Old Man and the Old Lady remembered his surname as Bitts (Josephine and Joe Crowshoe Sr. to Mike Ross, personal communication 1998). Betts's Indian name was Lame Bull. He was farm superintendent at the Blood Reserve and married Canon W.R. Haynes's daughter, Gertrude, in 1915 (Glenbow Archives, Gertrude Mary Margaret Betts fonds M89).

The white man said, "Oh, there's nothing." That night, while the white man was eating, a man came in. So he gave him a chair. He went to the door and closed it. [Soon] a rock rolled in. It hit the wall. The white man got up. He was going to pick up the rock but there was nothing. All night long he was being haunted by this man. In the morning the boys came. He told the boys, "Quit playing jokes on me. You were playing jokes on me all night."

The boys said, "It wasn't us, it's the bracelets. We'll go back to the burial site and put the bracelets back so at night they won't come back and bother you." So they went up to the hill and put the bracelets back. They buried them, came home. That night he slept well, nobody bothered him.

The next morning when the boys came there he said, "I really had a good sleep. Nobody bothered me."

So the boys told him, "Do you believe in ghosts now?"

And the white man said, "Yes, I do. I believe in ghosts." I've seen ghosts myself out here. They were walking. They didn't crawl under the fence, they just walked right through it. I looked. They didn't touch the ground.

JOSEPHINE: I got to tell you too. I heard. I was in the old school, not the new school. The old school had high stairs. The girls' playroom had high stairs and I heard this [sound], coming running down the stairs. I thought, "Here comes the matron." I opened the door to see the matron. [Almost whispering] Nooobody. But I heard somebody running down the stairs!

POKAAMOIKSI: BEES

MIKE ROSS, JOSEPHINE, AND REG CROWSHOE WERE IN BROCKET 27 OCTOBER 1998 WHEN THE OLD MAN, SPEAKING BLACKFOOT, RECOUNTED A DREAM HE HAD HAD. HE FIRST TOLD MIKE IN MAY 1996 THAT HE WANTED TO TELL THIS STORY. JIMMY STRIKES WITH A GUN TRANSLATED IN DECEMBER 1999.

Eight

JOE: Last night I had a dream about the bees. There was a Sun Dance and the cloth that they use in the centre-pole, the bees were taking those and making houses out of them. And there's a song that goes with the dream that I had [sings]. ...

A DREAM

THE OLD MAN, SPEAKING ENGLISH, TOLD THE FOLLOWING DREAM TO MIKE ROSS AND JOSEPHINE CROWSHOE ON 27 OCTOBER 1998.

JOE: Say, Mike, I had a dream. When I was sleeping I was drinking water. Somebody said, "I am the water, I am the water."

Another voice said, "I am the river, I am the river. Let the river flow, flow." That was my dream.

Nine

ℬROCKET

23 November 1998

MIKE ROSS RECORDED THE FOLLOWING ON 23 NOVEMBER 1998. JOSEPHINE WAS ALSO PRESENT. BLACKFOOT TRANSLATED BY JIM STRIKES WITH A GUN DECEMBER 1999.

LONGHORNS

JOE: [In Blackfoot] *Óki.* I'm going to talk about when the horses got sick here on the Peigan Reserve. A lot of good horses died because of the sickness. We cut the ears and we saved a lot of the good horses at that time. We used to go out there, split their ears, let them breathe [bleed?]. It saved lot of them. Horses died here. The horses died. There was this Old Man who had a lot of horses. His name was Many Horses. He knew how to cure horses; he knew the sicknesses.

[In English] Mike, long time ago the Peigans here had flu, epidemic flu. Sick. They die every day. I went to Pincher. I got vaccinate[d] here. [The Old Man rolled up his sleeve and showed his vaccination mark.]

[In Blackfoot] A long time ago they herded some longhorns through here. They came from the States. You can't get near them, they're really mean. We couldn't walk around out in the prairie. Those cows were really mean, they'd just chase. The chief and the councilmen met about the long-horned cattle that were grazing on the Peigan Reserve and they decided they weren't going to be grazed on the reserve anymore because they were too dangerous. ... It was in 1910, August, when the longhorn struck the Old Man in the ribs.

JOSEPHINE: I remember what he was saying, that time he was hooked by a longhorn on his side. This man I was talking about was a Nez Percé Indian. He married a woman from here, my grandmother. It was my father got him help. That was my father's father, that was my grandfather. [Josephine's grandfather, Joseph Warrior, married Suzette Can't Get a Horse.] He ran to the doctor to get him help and the doctor helped him, sewed him up. But he was okay. I remember my grandmother talking about it a little. She said, "I was helping him and my hands were all bloody." She said, "I ran to the creek to wash my hands. From the other side of the creek the people came. 'Did you get something?', like if they killed a cow they'd have something to eat. 'Did you kill any?' 'No. That was my husband that was hooked by a longhorn.'" These longhorns weren't from here. They were from the States somewhere and they brought them here so we'd look after them. But the Indian agent and the chiefs talked about them, and they didn't want them in here. It hurt the people.

A CLOSING PRAYER

THE FOLLOWING IS FROM THE OLD LADY'S CLOSING PRAYER AT "KUNATAITUPII: COMING TOGETHER ON NATIVE SACRED SITES," A NATIVE AND NON-NATIVE FORUM THAT WAS HELD AT WATERTON LAKES NATIONAL PARK, ALBERTA, ON 2–6 MAY 1990.

"The Indian woman that gave me my Indian name, gave me my Indian name when I was three years old. My Indian name is Pohkomaniitapatii. And she tied me, as we say in our Blackfoot way, she tied me, she gave me something to hold. These. I was going to put them on today but the string is hard to tie. They are beads, old beads, she gave me, she told me, the old woman that gave me my name, "These beads will give you a long life." I was three years old when I received them. My mother had them all these years. When she knows her end was coming she gave them to me and told me to hold them. ... Oh Great Spirit whose voice I hear in the winds, whose breath gives life to all the world hear me. I am small and weak. I need your strength and wisdom. Let me walk in beauty. Make my eyes behold the red and purple sunset. Make my hands respect the things that you have made. My ears sharp to hear your voice. Make me wise so that I may understand the things you have taught my people. Let me learn the lessons that you have hidden in every leaf and rock. I seek strength not to be greater than my brother but to fight my greatest enemy, myself. Make me almost ready to come to you with clean hands and straight eyes so that when life fades, like the fading sunset, my spirit may come to you without shame. Thank you." (Kunataipii, 1993: 275)

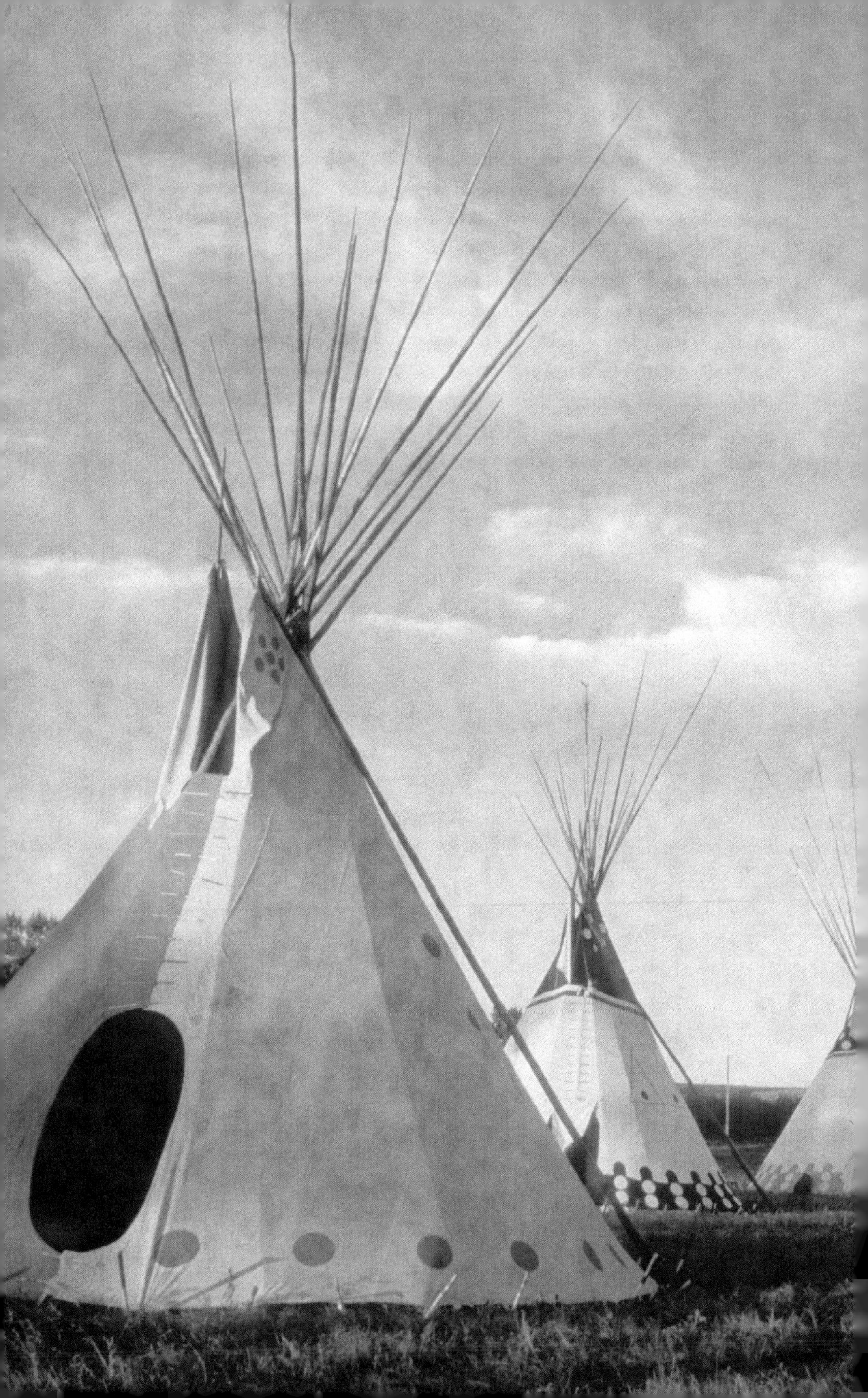

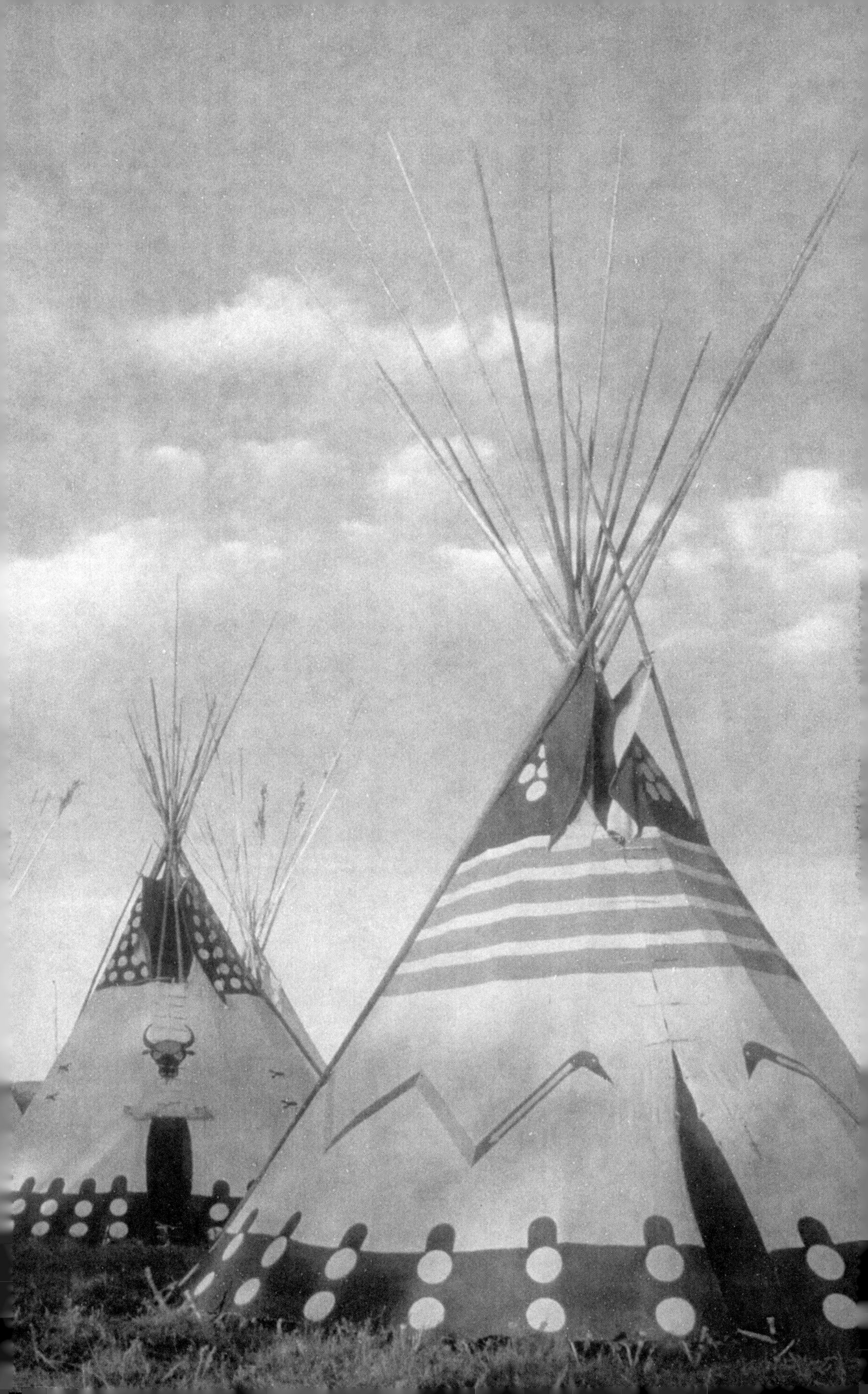

BIBLIOGRAPHY

Beahen, William, and Stan Horrall. *Red Coats On the Prairies*. Regina: Centax Books/PrintWest Publishing Services, 1998.

Blackfoot Gallery Committee (Glenbow Museum). *Nitsitapiisinni, The Story of the Blackfoot People*. Toronto: Key Porter Books, 2001.

Bohi, Charles W., and Lesli S. Kozma. *Canadian Pacific Western Depots: The Country Station in Western Canada*. David City, Nebraska: South Platte Press, 1993.

Brasser, Ted J. "Tipi Paintings, Blackfoot Style." *Contextual Studies of Material Culture*. Ed. David W. Zimmerly. Ottawa: National Museums of Canada, 1978.

Brink, Jack. "Dog Days in Southern Alberta." *Archaeological Survey of Alberta*, Occasional Paper No. 28. Edmonton: Alberta Culture, 1986.

Brownstone, Arni. *War Paint: Blackfoot and Sarcee Painted Robes in the Royal Ontario Museum*. Toronto: Royal Ontario Museum, 1993.

Canadian Art Club. *Indian Tribes of Canada: Edmund Morris*. Catalogue of exhibition, 1909.

Carter, Sarah. *Lost Harvests: Prairie Indian Reserve Farmers and Government Policy.* Montreal: McGill-Queen's University Press, 1990.

Crowshoe, Reg, and Sybille Manneschmidt. *Akak'stiman: A Blackfoot Framework for Decision-Making and Mediation Processes.* 2nd edition. Calgary: University of Calgary Press, 2002.

Dempsey, Hugh A. "The Snake Man." *Alberta History* 29: 4 (Autumn 1981), 1–5.

———. "The Blackfoot Indians," Pages 404–35 in *Native Peoples: The Canadian Experience.* Ed. R. Bruce Morrison and C. Roderick Wilson. Toronto: McClelland and Stewart, 1986.

———. "The Tragedy of Whitebird." *The Beaver, Hudson's Bay Company* 73: 1 (February–March 1993), 23–29.

———. *The Golden Age of the Canadian Cowboy: An Illustrated History.* Calgary: Fifth House Publishers, 1995.

Dempsey, James. "Persistence of a Warrior Ethic Among the Plains Indians." *Alberta History* 36: 1 (winter 1988), 1–10.

Ewers, John C. *The Blackfeet: Raiders on the Northwestern Plains.* Norman: University of Oklahoma Press, 1958.

———. *Indian Life on the Upper Missouri.* Norman: University of Oklahoma Press, 1968.

Fitz-Gibbon, Mary. *The Diaries of Edmund Montague Morris: Western Journeys 1907–1910.* Toronto: Royal Ontario Museum, 1985.

Fort Macleod History Book Committee. *Fort Macleod — Our Colourful Past*. Calgary: Fort Macleod Historical Society, 1977.

Frantz, Donald G., and Norma Jean Russell. *Blackfoot Dictionary of Stems, Roots, and Affixes*. 2nd edition. Toronto: University of Toronto Press, 1989.

Government of Canada. Annual Reports of the Royal North-West Mounted Police, Sessional Papers.

Government of Canada. Department of Indian Affairs, Reports on Boarding and Industrial Schools, Sessional Papers. 1904.

———. Department of Indian Affairs, Reports on Boarding and Industrial Schools, Sessional Papers. 1910.

Gray, James H. *A Brand of Its Own: The 100 Year History of the Calgary Exhibition and Stampede*. Saskatoon: Western Producer Prairie Books, 1985.

Haydon, A.L. *The Riders of the Plains: A Record of the Royal North-West Mounted Police of Canada, 1873–1910*. 1910; Edmonton: M.G. Hurtig, 1971.

Hellson, J.C., and M. Gadd. "Ethnobotany of the Blackfoot Indians." *Canadian Ethnology Service Paper*, No. 19. Ottawa: National Museums of Canada, 1974.

Hoffer, Samuel. *The Hutterites: Lives and Images of a Communal People*. Saskatoon: Hoffer Publishers, 1998.

Hungry Wolf (Gutohrlein), Adolf. *The Blood People: A Division of the*

Blackfoot Confederacy. New York: Harper and Row, 1977.

Hungry Wolf, Adolf and Beverly. *Pow-Wow*, vol. 1. Skookumchuk, BC: Good Medicine Books, 1983.

Hungry Wolf, Beverly. *The Ways of My Grandmothers*. New York: Quill, William Morrow and Company, 1982.

Johnston, Alex. *Plants and the Blackfoot*, Occasional Paper No. 15. Lethbridge: Lethbridge Historical Society, 1987.

Mandelbaum, David G. *The Plains Cree: An Ethnographic, Historical, and Comparative Survey*. 1940; Regina: Canadian Plains Research Centre, 1996.

Manneschmidt, Sybille. "Lives Lived: Joe Crowshoe." *Globe and Mail*. 6 January 2000: A16.

McClintock, Walter. *The Old North Trail: Life, Legends and Religion of the Blackfeet Indians*. 1910; Lincoln: A Bison Book, University of Nebraska Press, 1968.

———. *Old Indian Trails: An Authentic Look at Native American Life and Culture by the Adopted Son of a Blackfoot Chief*. 1923; Boston: Houghton Mifflin Company, 1992.

Meili, Dianne. *Those Who Know: Profiles of Alberta's Native Elders*. Edmonton: NeWest Press, 1991.

Milloy, John S. *A National Crime: The Canadian Government and the Residential School System, 1879 to 1986*. Winnipeg: University of Manitoba Press, 1999.

Nakano, Takeo Ujo. *Within the Barbed Wire Fence: A Japanese Man's Account of his Internment in Canada.* Toronto: University of Toronto Press, 1980.

Nuttall, Sue. "The Ghost House: Acculturation in Blackfoot Burial Patterns." *Philadelphia Anthropological Society Bulletin* 13: 2 (1960), 23-28.

"Obituary for Buffalo." *Lethbridge Herald.* 26 January 1981.

Obituary for McLaughlin (Judge) Frank Richard. *Lethbridge Herald.* 27 December 1993: D2.

Raczka, Paul. *Winter Count: A History of the Blackfoot People.* Brocket: Oldman River Cultural Centre, 1979.

Regular, Keith. "On Public Display." *Alberta History* 34: 1 (winter 1986), 1-10.

Ross, Michael, and Reg Crowshoe. "Shadows and Sacred Geography: First Nations History-Making from an Alberta Perspective." *Making Histories in Museums.* Ed. Gaynor Kavanagh. London: Leicester Press, 1996.

Scott-Brown, Joan. "The Short Life of St. Dunstan's Calgary Indian Industrial School, 1896-1907." *Canadian Journal of Native Education* 14: 1 (1987), 41-49.

Stepney, Philip H.R. "Director's Message: Repatriation of Canada's Heritage." *Storyteller, Alberta Culture, and Multiculturalism* 10: 3 (1990), 2.

Thomas, David, and Karin Ronnefeld, eds. *People of the First Man: Life Among the Plains Indians in Their Final Days of Glory.* New York: Promontory Press, 1982.

Waldman, Carl. *Who Was Who in Native American History: Indians and Non-Indians from Early Contact though 1900.* New York: Facts On File, Inc., 1990.

Walman, Ruth, and Susie Stahl. "Hutterite History: Past and Present" (unpublished paper). Saskatoon: Multicultural Youth Conference, 1985. Accessed at http://sesd sk.ca/grassroots/Riverview/page17.htm.

Wilson, Michael Clayton. "Bones of Contention: Treatment by Whites of Native Burials on the Canadian Plains." Pages 65–79 in *Kunatupii: Coming Together on Native Sacred Sites.* Eds. Brian O.K. Reeves and Margaret A. Kennedy. The Archaeological Society of Alberta, 1993.

Wissler, Clark. "Societies and Dance Associations of the Blackfoot Indians." *Anthropological Papers of the American Museum of Natural History* 11: 4. New York: American Museum of Natural History, 1913.

Wissler, Clark, and D.C. Duvall. *Mythology of the Blackfoot Indians.* 1908; Lincoln: A Bison Book, University of Nebraska Press, 1995.

INDEX

A

Aamsskáápipikani (Blackfeet or South Piegan) 19
Áápohsoy'yiis (Weasel Tail), see Crowshoe Sr., Joe, 19
aissko'kiinaiksi (ants), as metaphor for Hutterites, 199–200
Akak'stiman 163
Alberta Achievement Award 29
All-night Smoke ceremonies 28, 163
Anderton, T. George 181
Apisomakau (Running Wolf or Wolf Traveller) 43, 171–74
Ápistotooki (God) 118
Arthur, Chester A. (Indian Agent; Running Eagle) 147, *148*, 149
Arthur, Elizabeth Crocker *148*
Awakasina, see Crowshoe, Reg, 45
Awunna *109*

B

Back Fat, Philip *110*, *112*
Bad Eagle, Pat 93, *95*, 174, 175
Bastien, Bernard (Sam) *151*, 177
Bastien, George 177
Bear Child 102
Beaver Bundle Pipe 161
Bee Society 111
berry picking 105, 136
Betts, William (Lame Bull) 116, 203–204
Big Bull, Nap (Napoleon) 182–83, *184*
Big Bull, Willy 173
Big Plume *170*
Big Swan, Philip *151*, 186
Bird Woman (Sistsí) 102, *103*
bison 20, *24*
Black Chief *139*
Black Face *110*
Blackfoot (Siksiká)
    description of 19–26, 169–70
    language 19–20, 31–32, 54
    polygamy 103
Blackfoot Dictionary (Frantz and Russell) 32
Blackfoot Reserve 45, *61*, 86, 90, *110*

blacksmithing 57
Blood, *see* Káínaa, 19, *80*, 96, 186–87
Blood Reserve 90, 102, *179*
Brass, Morris 161
Brave Dog Society 28, 97, 102, 111, 117
Brings Down the Sun (Naato'siinapii; Running Wolf) 43, 60, 102, *103*, 106–108, *108*, 171
Brink, Jack 82
Brocket *38*, *39*, 51, *56*, 114, *151*
Brocket Trading Company *157*
Brownstone, Arni 106
Buffalo, Joe *151*
Buffalo, Laura Annie, *also see* Everybody Listens to the Thunder, 102
Buffalo Days 41
buffalo jump, *see* Head Smashed-In Buffalo Jump
Bull Plume 51, 122, *139*

C
Cadet Corps 64
Cadzow, Donald A. 47
Calgary Stampede 108, 157–58, 175, 195
Cambridge University 47
Canadian Citation for Citizenship 29
Canadian Pacific Railway 26
Canadian Rodeo Hall of Fame 108
Can't Get a Horse (Kata' inim' ahi), Suzette 40, 208
centre pole 83–85, *85*, 97
Chases Back Alone 60

Chicken Dance Society *39*, *110*
Calf, Chief 97
Chief in the Timbers (One Eye Jack) *48*
Christmas 52–53
Cranbrook 51, 52, 105–106
Crees 166–71
Creighton, Percy (Percy Shell Woman; Joe Martin) 111, *114*, 189–92
Crow Indian Reservation 139
Crow Agency 139
Crow Flag 57
Crow Flat, Mrs. *173*
Crow Shoe 101, *139*, 139
Crow Shoes, Willie *39*, 57, 96, 101–105, *105*, 109, *110*, 111–14
Crow Tail Feathers, *see* Noble, Brian, 46
Crowshoe, Evelyn 96–97, 180
Crowshoe, Jack *151*
Crowshoe Sr., Joe 27, 29, 43, 59, 70, 97, 132, 163, 164
on alcohol 117–18
birth and origin 35, 101–102
ceremonialist 21–22, 26–31, 42–45, 93
childhood 46, 56, 57, 73–75, 129–31, 145–46, 149–58
China 67–71
Christianity 28, 41, 57–58, 75, 120–23, 159–63, 184–85
death of 33
dreams 205
during the Depression 127–29
Gobi Desert 69–71

Indian agents 60, 147–49, 182–83
residential school 122–23, 152–56
tipis 28, 38–39, *120*
Crowshoe, Josephine
    (Pohkomaniitapatii [From Far
    Away Nez Percé Woman]) 28, *30,*
    30, 138
    death of 141
    initiation as a Holy Woman 97
    origins 40, 141, 177, 208
Crowshoe, Reg 27–28, *29*, 35, 96, 170
Crowshoe, Rose 27
Cuthand, Stan 161
CY Ranch 101, 102, 105

D

Daines, Duane 130
dancing 49–51
David, Willie *151*
Davis, Charlie (Doesn't Cook) 105,
    186–87, *188*, 191–92
Deer Chief, see Crow Shoes, Willie 101
Dempsey, Hugh 90, 105
disease 25
dogs 79
Doucet, Father Léon *107*, 108

E

Eagle Tail Feathers (Ak-Si-Na),
    Mortimer *48*
Edwards, Henrietta Muir 42
Edwards, Oliver Cromwell *42*, 42

Elk-dog, see horses and *Ponokáómitaa*,
    79
English, John *151*
English, Julius 45
Everybody Listens to the Thunder
    (Ekistinopa, All Listening;
    Laura Annie Buffalo) 101–102,
    190
Ewers, John C. 168
Ex Terra Foundation 67, 69
Explorations in Western America,
    1784–1812 (Thompson) 80

F

face paint 163
farming 25, 54–56, 56, 64, 75, *124*, 124–26
First Rider, George 187
Fish Eaters 178
Fish Wolf Robe 96
food 21, 41, 49, *50*, 135
Fort Macleod 26, 42, *74*, 128, *131*, 156,
    181, 202
Fort Peck Indian Reservation 166
Four Horns 171–73, *173*

G

Gaigen, Sgt. *139*
gambling 86–90
gender 23–24
ghosts 75, 136–37, 202–204
ghost houses 202–203
Glenbow Museum 32, 122

221

Good Chaser 96
Good Young Man 139
Goodrider, Charles 112
Graham, Mr. (Indian Agent; Rock Buffalo) 116
Grassy Water 46, 47
Green Grass Bull 139
Grier, Charlie 186

H
Harper, Elijah 187, 189
Haynes, Elizabeth (Weasel Woman) 116
Haynes, Gertrude (Deer Woman) 116, 203
Haynes, W.R. 51, 116, 123
Head Smashed-In Buffalo Jump 35, 41–42, 42, 43, 69
Head Smashed-In Buffalo Jump Interpretive Centre 41
Heavy Shield 110
Highway 3 26
Hind Bull 96
Hogbin, George H. 112
Hogbin, Mrs. G.H. 112
Holy Fox Woman 97
Hoof, Philip 105
Horn Society 102, 111
horses 60, 63, 64, 70, 76, 79–82, 80, 105, 130–34, 177, 178–80, 187
 introduction of 23–24, 80
Hudson's Bay Company Store 75, 129, 130

Hungry Wolf, Adolf 55, 178
hunting 20, 78, 105–106, 134–35
Hutterites 199–200, 201

I
Iron Shirt 51
Itsipiawayaki 43

J
Japanese Canadians 68
Joseph, Chief 40

K
Káínaa, *see also* Blood, 19, 20, 32
Ki'somm (Ki-sóum) 178
Knowlton, James 112
Kootenay Indian Reserve 51–53
Kootenays 51
Ktunaxa (formerly Kootenays First Nations) 51, 53

L
LaGrandeur, Pete 108, 133
Lancaster, Mr. (Indian Agent; Rider) 116
Lawrence, Herbert (Small Eyes) 161
Little Leaf, Jim 151, 186
Little Plume 139
livestock 58–60, 63–64, 105, 125, 207–208
Lone Fighters 169–70
Long Hair (White Hair) 101–102, 175, 176, 178, 187
Lost Harvests (Carter) 25

M

Man Who Smokes 186–87
Manneschmidt, Sybille 163
Many Chiefs 96, 187
Many Feathers, Nathan 96, *112*
Many Guns *173*
Many Guns, Mrs. *173*
Many Horses 207–208
Many Rifle Man 46–47
Many Shot Number 2 *110*
Marsden, W.D. 90
Mason, D. *48*
McClintock, Walter 22, 103
McKay, George 114
McKenzie, Malcolm *170*
McLaughlin, Richard "Judge" 150
Meat Face, Edward 150, *151*
medicine 23, 109–110
Medicine Calf, Joe *151*
Medicine Pipe 111, 184
medicine pipe bundle, *see also* Thunder Medicine Pipe, 27–28, 40
Meili, Dianne 134
Morris, Edmund 45, 106, 108
Morning Bull, Jim *151*
mosquitoes (*Ksisohksisiiksi*) 164
Mosquito Society 111

N

Naatoas (Sun Dance headdress) 28, 96, *103*, 138, *173*, 175, 178
Naatoyinaimsskaaii 102

Nam'itsi'piaki (Went in There for No Reason) 43
Nash, Harry 25
National Aboriginal Achievement Award for Heritage and Spirituality 31
Natoo'kinimaki (Catching Them Two at the Time Woman) 43
Natoo-si iniipa, *see also* Brings Down the Sun, 43
Nez Percé 40, 79, 208
Nez Percé War 40
Niitsítapiiksi (real people) 19, 20, 23
Noble, Brian 35, 46, 67–68
North Peigan, Victor *151*
North West Mounted Police, see also Royal North-West Mounted Police 25, 57, *105*, *139*, *181*

O

Oblates of Mary Immaculate (OMI) 108
Okan, Sun Dance of the Blackfoot 90
Old Bulls Society 111
Oldman River 26, 37, 46–49, 166
One Gun *110*
Onespot, John *112*
Onion Lake, SK 47
Order of Canada 31

P

Pard, Alan 114
Pard, Albert 58

Peigans 82–83, 166–71, 203, 207
Peigan Reserve 25, 42, 47, *51*, *56*, *73*, 108, 112, 114, *116*
  description of 26, 54–55, 60
  livestock 207–208
  jail 56, 63
Plain Eagle, Margaret 114
Plume, Larry 93, 96
Piikáni, *see also* Peigans, 19, 25–26
Piikáni Nation Council 44
Pincher Creek 26, 36, 40, 59, 63, 108, 150
Pippy, Charles F. *112*
Plain Eagle, Pat 187
Pollard, Harry 110
ponokáómitaa (Elk-dog), *see also* horses, 79–82
Poplar, Montana 166
Porcupine Hills 26, 54, *55*
Potts, Jerry *139*
powwows 31, 37, 45, 60, 93–95, 139
Prairie Chicken, Arnold 150
Pretty Rider 93
Pretty Young Man *110*

R

Race Horse Society 39, 111, 186, 189
Rattlesnake Calf Shirt 86–92, *87*
  origin of rattlesnake power 90
Red Coat Society 28
Red Men 60
Red Top, Chief (Stokinota; Chief Butcher; Stooping Over Butcher; Leans Over Butchering; Chief Straight Hair) 166–71, *170*
Red Wolf 58
Red Young Man *151*
Reevis, Charlie, *see* Sooie, *179*
Regular, Keith 158
residential schools 26, 122
Rides-at-the-Door *91*, *92*, 100, 168, 189
Rides-at-the-Door, Mrs. *96*, 138
rodeos 58–60, 77–78, 132
Roman Catholic Sacred Heart Residential School 108, 112
Royal Canadian Mounted Police 57
Royal North-West Mounted Police 57, 105
Running Eagle *139*
Running Wolf (Brings Down the Sun) 104, *137*
Runs Among Buffalo *139*

S

sacred objects, *see* centre pole, medicine pipe bundle, *Naatoas*, tipis, topknot, 27–28
  role of women 137
  transfer ceremonies 37, 42, 95
Sacred Owl *151*
Sarcee Man *47*, *48*
Scott-Brown, Joan 112
Scraping White, Willie 111, *112*, 114
Scriver Collection *30*, 30
Shining Double *139*

224

Short Thunder Medicine Pipe 27, 43, 92–93, 95–96
  bundle lineage 96
Skunk, Bob 93
Siksiká (Blackfoot) 19, 51, *110*, 161
Sistts'i (Little Bird) 43
Small Legs, Jim *151*
Smithsonian Institution 47, 64
societies 111
Sooie (Charlie Reevis) 96, 119, *179*
Spider Ball *110*
St. Dunstan's Calgary Industrial School 57, 110, *112*, 112
St. Peter's Anglican mission *184*
St. Peter's Church of England 114
Starlight, James *112*
Steed, Ernst 64
Stocken, Percy *112*
Straight Hair (Chief Butcher) 109, 166
Strikes With A Gun, Charlie *151*, 202
Striped Squirrel 111
Sugar, Frank *110*
Sun Dance (*Ookáán*) 21, 28, 37, 60, 61, 62, 85, 137–38, 139, 163, 173, 174, 175–80, *176*, *179*, *181*
  prohibition of 138
  revival of ceremony 96–97, 137–38, 180
Sun Dance Cane Woman 187
sweat lodge 68, 144–45, *145*
sweetgrass 95
Swims Under, Mike 60, *61*, 61, 96, 180
Swims Under, Mrs. 63

T

Taber 68
tea dance *142*
Three Persons, Tom 175
Thunder Medicine Pipe, *see* Short Medicine Pipe 37, 39, 42, 44, 45, 116–17
Thunder Medicine Pipe Society 28, 95
Timber Limits 54, 58, 78
tipis 28–39, 64–65, 68, *118*, 194
  designs 38, 39, 45, 46, 53, 186–97, *193*, *197*
  transfer 186–97
Tobacco Plains 106
topknot 37
Tough Bread *48*
Treaty 7 25, 45, 54, 111

U

University of Alberta 42
University of Calgary 29
University of Montana 29

V

Victoria Jubilee Home Indian Residential School 72, *74*, 73–76, 122–23, *151*, 153–56, *153*
  deaths at 75, 122

W

Warrior (Soo Woo), Joseph 40, 208
Warrior, Lucy (née Yellowhorn) 177

Warrior, Sam 177

Waterton 83, 208

Ways of My Grandmother, The (Hungry
    Wolf) 20, 96

Weadick, Guy 175

Weasel Walker, Paul 161

Weaselhead, Pat 96

Wells, Jim 176

Where Crow Eagle Dances 49

Where We Drowned 90–92

whiskey (*náápiaohkii*) 24

White Bird, Chief 40

White Cow 48

Wilson, Robert Nathaniel (Inuskaisto
    or Long-Faced Crow) 55

winter count 23, 51, 122

Wolf Fighter (Teddy Bastein) 97

Wolf Flats 46, 101, 105, 114, 174

Y

Yellow Creek 105

Yellow Horn, Chief Tom 151

Yellow Horn Jr., Tom 151

IN SOUTHERN ALBERTA

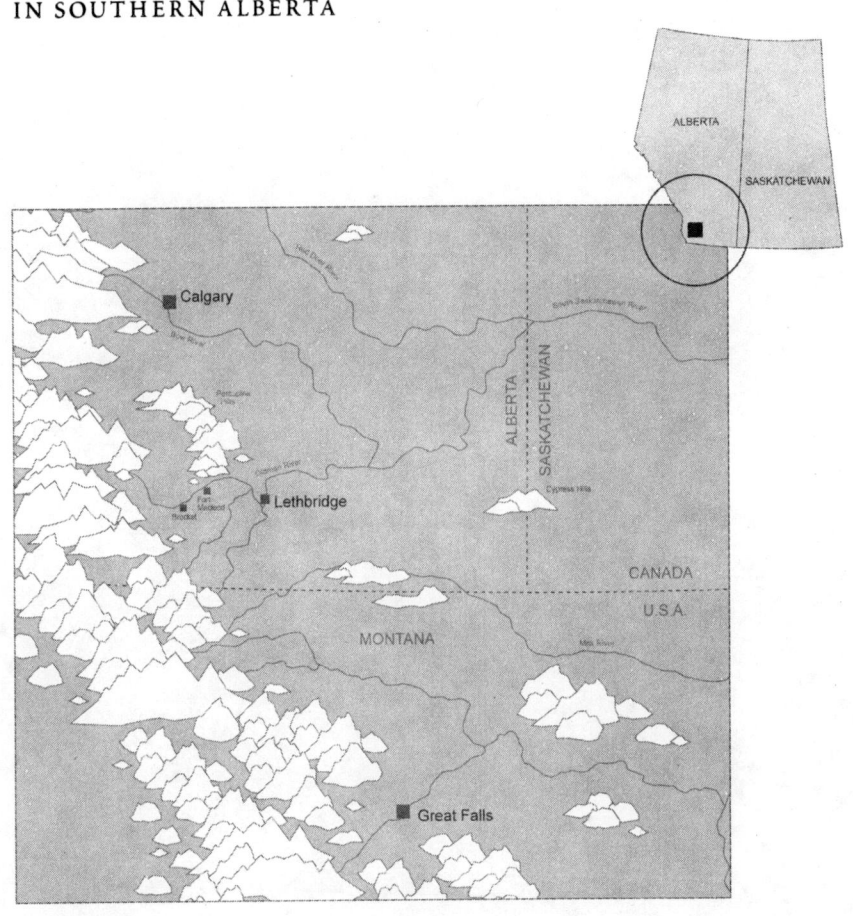

ON THE PEIGAN INDIAN RESERVE

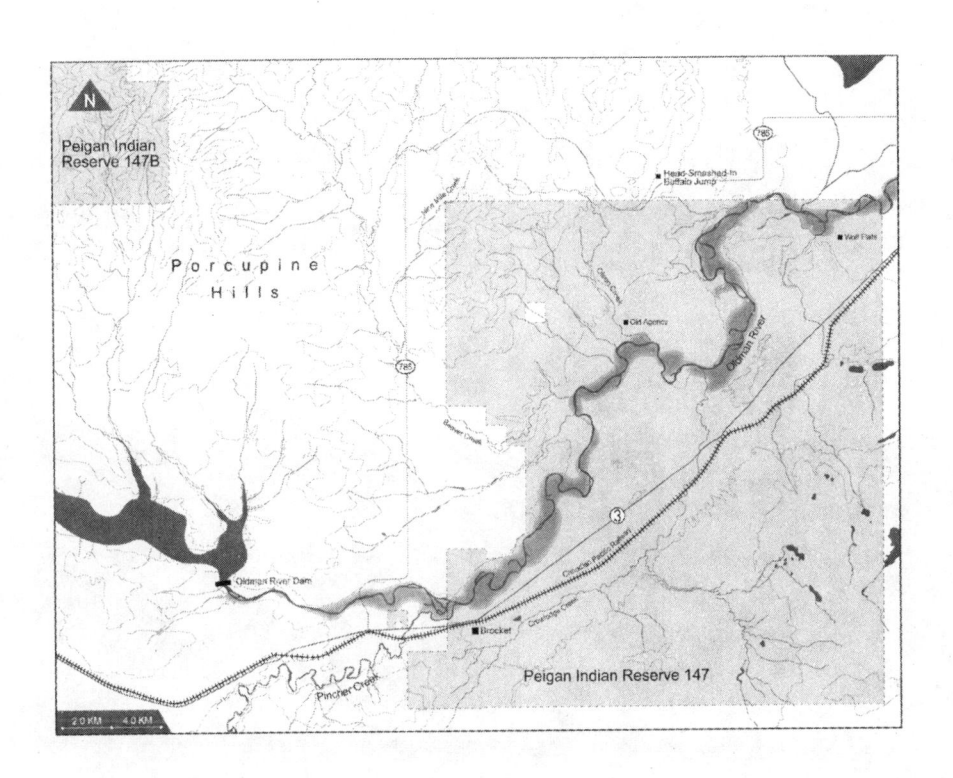

AT BROCKET

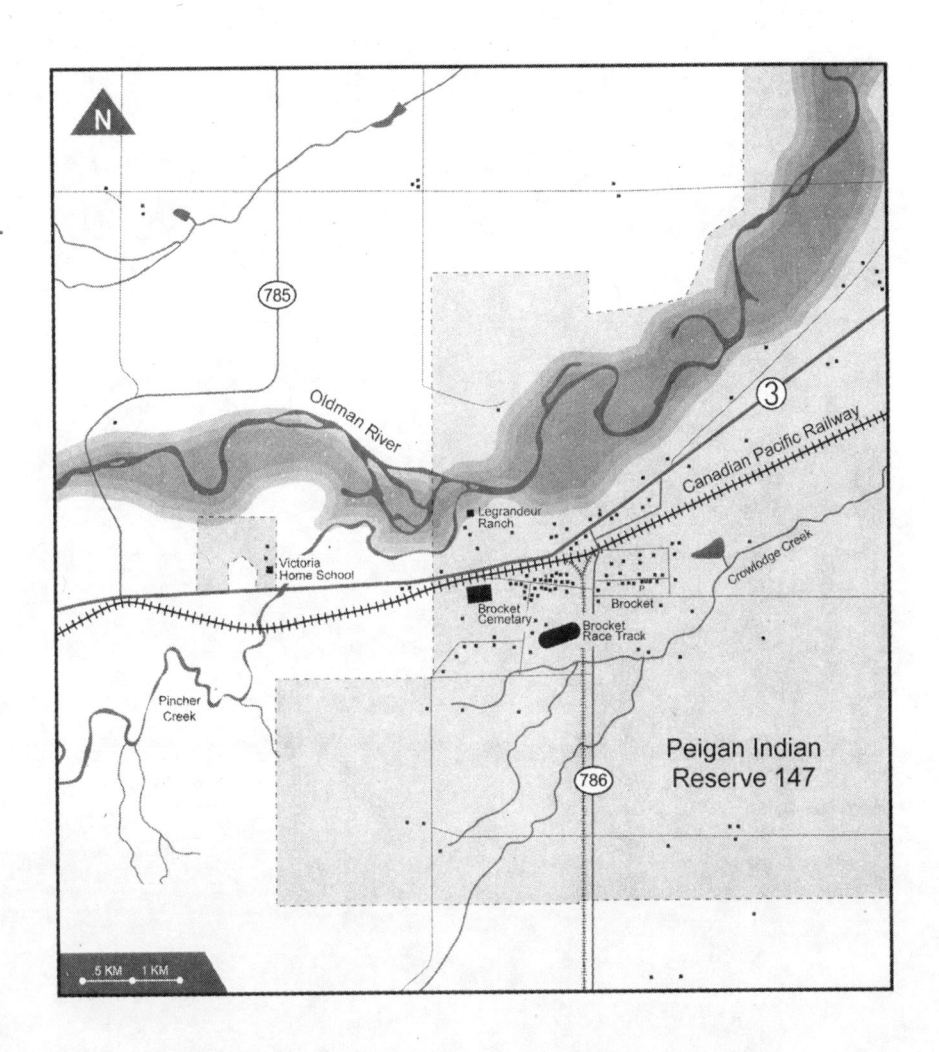

Michael Ross is a retired park planner and heritage resources consultant living in Edmonton, Alberta. He has degrees from the University of California at Berkeley (Geology) and the University of Leicester in England (Museum Studies). Several years of travelling, working, and photographing throughout western North America, Mexico, and Spain were driven by a slowly developing muscle disease that eventually forced him to stop working in 2001. He met the Crowshoes in 1989, attended numerous cultural ceremonies, and later agreed to help the "Old Man" write his book — a vow that took eleven years to fulfill.

¶ To serve its complex hierarchies, the text is set in three typefaces: Minion Pro, Cronos Pro, and Poetica. All three were designed by Robert Slimbach.

spur out of the bundle to
fied, she right away remember
let it was wrapped in — the
It was a pendleton blanket
present when the blanket
he part of the bundle — in
s   when the country was so
No one could afford a
n blanket, nor had any way
 the company mill in pendleton
By some miracle the bundle
had managed to get there
k. Now the blanket formed
r wrapping of the bundle
frayed, dirty, with holes
s worn into it. Then it was
such blanket in the country
It was special   she remember